mud
MOUNTAIN

Atulya K Bingham

mud
MOUNTAIN

Aklya K Bingham

mud
MOUNTAIN

Atulya K Bingham

www.themudhome.com

mud
MOUNTAIN

A MUDHOUSE BOOK

First edition published in the UK in 2017.

Copyright © Atulya K Bingham 2017.

The right of Atulya K Bingham to be identified as the author of this work has been asserted in accordance with sections 77 and 78 of the Copyright Designs and Patents Act 1988.

No part of this publication may be reproduced, stored in a retrieval system, or transmitted in any form or by any means, electronic, mechanical, photocopying, recording, or otherwise, without prior written permission of the copyright owner.

This book is sold subject to the condition that it shall not, by way of trade or otherwise, be lent, re-sold, hired out or otherwise circulated in any form of binding or cover other than that in which it is published and without a similar condition including this condition being imposed on the subsequent purchaser.

ISBN 9781787230644

Cover photograph by Melissa Maples.

Dedicated to the readers of The Mud Home.
Because if you weren't reading, I wouldn't be writing.

Acknowledgements

First, I thank my parents for bringing me up with a healthy love of the outdoors and an open-minded attitude toward spirituality.

Much appreciation as usual to Dudu and the late Celal for being the best neighbours an eccentric witch like me could ask for. Also, gratitude is due to all the folk who have got their hands dirty on my spot of land over the past four years. There are so many of you. A particularly earthy hug goes out to my Mud brother Kieran for rock shifting, teaching me the art of pre-nailing, dragging his friends over to work and generally being a helpful soul. As always a huge thank you to Dad for his ongoing support in all ways. Much love to Yvonne Bartfeld for holding the doors of the spirit world open over the years, and to Birgit Sabinsky for her unwavering belief in me, and the nurturing of my creative spirit. A special mention goes to Jo Vaisey for the best Yorkshire puddings this side of Doncaster.

Regards The Mud Mountain Blog, I'd like to thank the gifted Melissa Maples once again for her generosity in sharing her stunning photographs. Brian Crocker has also shared many of his bright ideas with me.

Thank you once again to Helen Baggott for her careful edit of the text.

Due to a lack of funds and an inability to graft within the system, in May 2011 Atulya K Bingham found herself camping alone on a remote Turkish hill. There was no power or water on the land. She knew almost nothing about outdoor survival either. It was the start of an adventure that profoundly changed her beliefs about what is enjoyable, or possible. In 2012 Atulya began to document her experiences in *The Mud Mountain Blog*. This is an edited collection of those articles posted between 2012 and late 2016.

2012

The Beginning

September 2012

Why would anyone move into a tent and live on a mountain for eight months? A mountain with no power, no water, and no permanent shelter to speak of.

Something has to have gone wrong.

The trouble all began with a dream, and in many ways it ended with one too. Only it was a dream I had never planned. One I hadn't expected at all.

I'm lucky enough to own a small plot of land. It sits snug within the pomegranate-laden folds of Turkey's Mediterranean. I stare out at great hulks of mountain pitching themselves into the sea. The surrounding pine thickets whir in the balmy breeze, while buzzards loop through the blue overhead. My nearest neighbour is four hundred metres away. It's so quiet, when she speaks on the phone I hear her every word.

It could have been very different, though. For not so long ago, I harboured a few grandiose plans for this spot of land. Back in the beginning of 2011, this 2500 square metres of the planet was to be transformed into a living, breathing vision; a meditation centre. It was a fantasy I had cherished for years, and I'd already had one bash at manifesting it further along the coast in the Kabak valley. I had failed spectacularly. But I'm a headstrong sort, and not much prone to heeding advice. It's the kind of personality that either does very well or very badly, depending on the circumstances.

I wasn't the only one set on this vision either. Seth and Claire, two friends from South Africa, had recently flown in to join me in the venture. They were fellow teachers and yogis, and as such we seemed to be a dream-team; a fantastic, three-pronged super-group. We had been planning our centre for months, right down to the size of the gong at the entrance.

Spring was damp and cool that year, summer late in coming. The winter grass that adorns the steep hills of Turkey's Mediterranean rolled in thick, green waves. There was still quite a bite to the gusts of sea air blowing in too, and they slapped the cobalt water whipping it into unpredictable shapes. Seth, Claire and I set up a temporary base in the nearby seaside village of Alakır and looked forward to attacking our project. Sometimes, however, life has other plans.

From the beginning, it seemed nothing would work out for us. The first setback was that we couldn't manage to lay our hands on a car. Or motorcycle. Or licences. So for all intents and purposes, we were grounded, stuck twiddling our thumbs a good half an hour drive from the land. It gave us plenty of time to think. And talk. For reasons no one could quite put their finger on, doubts seeped in between the cracks of our plans. As the weeks groaned by, a vague but unsettling cloud of unease began to spread through our close-knit triangle. I wondered what to do.

Then, without warning a guide appeared. He trotted out from the aphotic depths of the Lycian forests one cold evening in late March. Brian was a hiker. He had the wild look all those who spend too long in the Lycian mountains finally acquire – a look I myself would soon absorb. He could often be found a thousand-odd metres above sea level, cooking rogan josh over a campfire with a copy of Heidegger's *Basic Writings* in his back pocket. With his shock of white hair, caustic laugh, and sawing Australian vowels, he was what you might call 'a character'.

I perched on a beanbag next to the fire. Brian pulled himself closer to the wood-burner. He took sporadic sips out of his mug of tea and held it neatly on his lap when he was done. He narrowed his eyes before imparting his portentous message.

"Well, Doll, looks like you need to get yourself a tent and spend a night alone on that land. Let the Earth speak to you," he said.

I rubbed my hands over the stove and nodded. "Of course, let Mother Nature talk to me. Listen to Gaia and all of that."

Yet inwardly I baulked. Really? Did I have to listen? Couldn't I just have a fabulous plan, make colourful scribbles in my notebook and get on with it? It seemed so uncomfortable, inconvenient, time consuming; trekking all the way up to the land and freezing my butt off for a night. There was no toilet, no running water. And there were all the possibilities of trouble, too. Wild boar were common in the forests, lascivious locals even more widespread. It would be a night fraught with fear and insomnia, no doubt. Nonetheless, something in me must have seen merit in the idea, because a few days later I was scouring the house for a tent. All that I could lay my hands on was a Wendy House, the type small children use for den-making in the back garden.

Beggars can't be choosers, they say. The next day I packed the Wendy House into a small yellow day pack, along with a blanket and a bin-liner. I filled the pockets with dried apricots and nuts, and a bottle of water. Off I went. Off to hear my land. The plot was a good fifteen to twenty kilometres from Alakır bay, and I'd set out far too late. The sun was edging past noon as I trotted along the water's edge, the sea collecting flecks of gold in its wavy pockets.

When I reached the end of the beach, I spotted a tractor approaching. I flagged it down. Hurling my pack into the cement-caked trailer, I climbed in. It was a dusty, lurching ride, but it got me a good part of the way into the valley. Once we reached the mosque, its stone minaret searching for the sky in the midst of a forest of crowding pines, I jumped out.

Two hours of hiking later, I was closing in on the unfamiliar territory of my land. As I ambled along the dirt track, I passed gaggles of village women squatting on their front steps in their bloomers and headscarves. Some were toothless, many were wrinkled, all wore smiles and hooted their hellos at me. Bolstered by the good feeling, I clambered through the thin boundary of holly trees and pines to breach my square of earth.

Finally, I'd made it. I was here. On my own turf. I pricked my ears up and did my utmost to listen to what, if anything, that spot of turf was saying. All I could make out was a few birds twittering and insects buzzing.

The first question was where to set up camp. I trudged up the slope, while grass stalks, thick and lush, brushed my ankles and calves. I scoured left and right for signs.

"Come on! I'm here. Speak!" I muttered at the undergrowth. Nothing. Just the wind gently rattling the pine needles above.

Soon, I reached a small plateau at the top of the land. Here it was utterly overgrown, hemmed in by an army of barbed thorn bushes. One corner was sheltered by three magnificent old olive trees, their gnarled trunks wrangled into knotty sculptures. I dropped my pack, rubbed my shoulders, and paced about, relishing the feeling of wandering about a piece of the Earth I could call my own. My domain. It's an incredibly visceral sensation to own land. Frighteningly instinctive. I heard the quiet but unmistakable growl of something primal inside me, and to be honest I didn't completely approve.

Strolling past the spikes of the thorn bushes, I stopped for a moment. They were far from attractive, their pale green claws splayed in messy clumps. Still, I couldn't escape the sensation there was more to them. They were natural barbed wire and as such offered a protection. It was a peculiar circle of safety, and I realised a pig or human would have trouble getting through it. Looking up, I saw three olive trees towering over me, their arms outstretched like old family, or ancestors or something. It was then that I noticed, I was grinning to absolutely no one at all.

This was it. I'd found my spot.

It wasn't difficult to erect the tent. The thing was made for a seven-year-old, after all. I crawled inside, but I could neither sit up nor lie down. It was too small. The best I could do was lay flat and let my legs poke out of the flap at the front. I just hoped and prayed no scorpions were prowling, and hoped again it didn't rain.

Nature is fascinating when you get into it, though. It looks so dirty and menacing from the smudge-free windows of a city. Yet once you're in it, you forget all of that, because the earth is speckled with stardust. Green magic spills out from every niche. As the sun drifted over the top of the mountains, I felt excitement rather than dread. The Wendy House, the smell of the grass, the twisting trunks of the trees, the open sky, all of them called back long-forgotten childhood moments in the outdoors, times before a rational education had stuffed reality into meaningless boxes, times when magic had been a living possibility.

As twilight moved through the trees, I decided to build a fireplace. Soon enough, I was gazing at clouds of orange sparks flying through the darkness, while munching on those apricots. One by one, the stars pushed through the night sky. I looked about, listening, still waiting for the land to speak. It was then, as I perched on a rock lost in the hypnotic dance of the flames that I heard them. The Land. And the Sky.

They were talking.

Can The Earth Talk?

November 2012

Can the Earth talk? Isn't it just a great ball of mud rocketing about an even bigger ball of combustibles? Surely it's only humans that have feelings and sensitivity and the like. All this claptrap about Gaia, isn't it just a long deep wallow in unabashed anthropomorphism?

At the time of my first night in the Wendy House on my land back in 2011, I wasn't exactly a materialist. But I was hardly an Earth Mother either. I'd already lived in the countryside for a few years. I'd seen the blood-curdling displays nature could indulge in. There were ghastly critters, scorpions, poisonous snakes, even ants morphed into sinister armies when they banded together to devour a moth alive. All in all, life on planet Earth appeared to be a wheel of ferocious struggle; a relentless and exhausting scrabble to stay alive and avoid seemingly inevitable pain. I loved the beauty nature offered, but I was unconvinced of her underlying ethics. That night, as I stabbed at my campfire with a broken pine branch and felt the sweet apricots squelch between my teeth, I sensed the primitive in all her rawness.

In fact, unbeknown to me at the time, there has been a batch of research regarding the sensitivity of our planet and the various life forms that dwell on her. None is more fascinating than the investigations into the secret life of plants. Long before the New Age donned its rose-tinted spectacles, a while before the more cynical post-moderns too, people were researching the feelings of plants. Back in 1848 a certain Gustav Theodor Fechner showed that plants responded to talk and affection.

This theory was backed up by the Bengali polymath Sir Jagadesh Chandra Bose,[1] who discovered in 1900 that plants seemed to suffer from spasms when administered poison or subjected to other aggressive behaviour. More alarmingly, he found the same responses in metals too, which generated something of a kerfuffle. Then, later on in the sixties, the independent scientist James Lovelock, published his Gaia hypothesis. He argued that the Earth is a self-regulating, interacting organism, with all entities on the planet being compared to the separate cells and organs that make up a body. The environmentalists almost completely adopted the theory. But back in the realm of positivist science, doors began swiftly swinging shut. Bose, Fechner and Lovelock are still greeted by the academic community with steely stares of scepticism. According to the mainstream, it's all pseudoscience; emotional, childish poppycock.

I'm not a scientist. I'm a human being. Being human is a fascinating state of play. All of us are perched upon this spinning green orb trying to deduce what the hell is going on around us. But whether we rely on our five senses, our logic, our emotions or intuition, we can never know beyond all reasonable doubt. Because there is always reasonable doubt. Can we be sure that simply because an organism doesn't have a brain, that it doesn't possess sensitivity? Can we be certain that a

---

[1] Sir Jagadish Chandra Bose, CSI, CIE, FRS, also spelled Jagdish and Jagadis, was a Bengali polymath, physicist, biologist, biophysicist, botanist and archaeologist, and an early writer of science fiction

massive body such as our planet doesn't have some sort of sentience? We can't. We can't because our modes of understanding the world in which we live (senses, logical analysis, intuition) are limited. We can't even prove we didn't make the entire world up or that we're not living permanently in a dream.

So back to the rocks and the campfire and the Wendy House that was too small for me to fit my legs in. Back to that magical night, my first night alone on my land in the Turkish hills. There I was, staring into a fire feeling distinctly cavewoman. The burning wood hissed. The thick pines overhead murmured. Above me stars and constellations I had no idea of the name of winked and pulsated like distant lighthouses. The huge dark gulf of the infinite was out there. Space, and more space, and more. And yet here I was, this pondering human ape, my rump of flesh and blood wedged firmly onto the Earth's crust, looking up and sensing the awe of a fathomless night sky.

Gaia doesn't speak to us in a deep booming voice. She doesn't send messages crashing into us with lightning bolts or flashing lights. But whenever you hear the whisper of the breeze, the rippling of birdsong, the approaching bellow of a storm or the rhythmic whirring of crickets, Gaia is communicating. It isn't logical. I agree with the academics. The experience is very unfashionably emotional.

I smelt the dampness of the dew on the grass. The hard ridges on my rock pushed into me. I heard an owl call out into the forest, other foreign rustlings in the grass. This is what I understood as Gaia speaking, and what I realised is that she was talking to me in a code of feelings. The message I received was clear. It was the feeling of belonging, of being finally well and truly home. As the darkness pulled in about me, it dawned on me that I hadn't ever felt so intensely a part of a place before.

There may be a multitude of explanations for the way I felt that night. But in all honesty, does it really make any difference? Because however much Western society represses or belittles emotions, it is feelings, not logic which actually direct people's lives. And if they don't, well what miserable grey existences they are. Love is replaced by marital contracts, family bonds become obsolete, we cart grandma off to an institution and live in faceless boxes instead of inspiring hand-crafted cottages. Life without feeling really isn't life at all. Indeed, it is perhaps pertinent to wonder, if the planet really is no more sentient than a concrete block of flats why do we all get so emotional about it. If the Earth has no more soul than a strip of asphalt, then why walking on the former invigorates and rejuvenates us, while the latter drains and demoralizes us. There are few things that are universally true from culture to culture, but a feeling of well-being in nature is one of them.

So, yes I admit it defied all logic. It was irrational and unscientific. It might have been a figment of my mind. If my senses were to be believed I was sitting with my arse in the dirt, high up on a lonesome mountain slope without a roof over my head. Logic and memory both informed me that there were wild boar, scorpions and snakes all about. Yet my emotions were telling another story altogether. They told me I was more at home here than I had ever been in my life. I felt strangely taken care of, nurtured even.

I decided there and then. Somehow I had to live up there.

The Most Important Thing

December 2012

The perspiration dripped from my face as I pushed the wheelbarrow. The earth track that led down to my land was scarred with ruts and craters. The barrow wheels wedged themselves into each one. Every time they did I had to pull the weighty metal cart out of the hole and take a run at the offending hillocks. At the entrance to the property a stony path plunged through a mess of brambles. On reaching the incline, the barrow promptly gained a mind of its own, rattling out of control down the slope. I galloped after it, hanging onto the handlebars for dear life, suffering scratches and stubbed-toes for the duration. I clung, because that wheelbarrow held within it the most important thing in my life. In fact it held the most important thing in the whole world. I now realised only too well exactly how fundamental that thing was because my land seemed to possess none of it. That treasure was water.

One way or another I've endured a trying relationship with water throughout my life. Either there's too much of the stuff or too little. I've been on the wrong end of floods, terminally dripping ceilings, furred up water pipes, wild boar bashing through pipelines and now, very conspicuously I was in a drought. There was no running water on my land. There were no streams or well springs either. It was May, and I had one more rainfall to go before summer took the Mediterranean in its fiery, waterless grip. Everyone said living on my mountain would be impossible.

"Olmaz!" came the cries from all quarters. *Olmaz* is Turkish and translates roughly as, "You can't or shouldn't do it."

Did I mention that I was a headstrong sort? That it had its pros and cons? It's the bane of my life, but when someone barks the word "can't" at me, I find myself driven by this insatiable bent to defy them.

It was now nearly a month after my first auspicious night on the land. I'd hired a car to transport as much of a camp up to the mountain as I could. However, the track was in such a state of dusty furrowed imperfection, the little Fiat Punto proved ill-equipped to descend all the way to the land itself. I had parked it a hundred metres uphill. Bit by bit I wheeled or carried down a tent, mattress, sleeping bag, rucksack of clothes, a pick, rake, spade, scythe, washing-up bowl, teapot, and now a 30 litre plastic tank of water. How long would 30 litres last? I wondered. Well, that all depends on how you use it.

And you use it a lot. An awful lot. With the obvious exception of oxygen, water's the thing we rely on most in the world. H2O. Liquid diamonds. If you're breathing, you need it.

As I scanned the huge grasses and thickets of spines my first task loomed in front of me. I had to clear a space for my tent. Eyeing my three new garden tools, I wondered which to choose. It may or may not surprise you to learn I had zero experience with DIY or gardening when I moved onto the land that summer. I couldn't even bang nails in. I'd never planted a seed. The only thing I could lay claim to was having taken part in some terracing. The Mediterranean coast is riddled with rocks, which, when you know how to use them, prove incredibly useful. First the stones are dug out with a pick and used to form a wall. After that the earth is raked forwards to create a level surface. It's a timeless system that's been employed since the ancient Greeks. The only trouble is, it's very thirsty work. I looked at my small plastic water container. It looked back at me impassively.

I grabbed the scythe and hacked away at the rampant undergrowth, dry grasses and thorns that came up to my shoulders. Then began my first foray into the art of terracing. After a few rock-crushed fingers and the onset of blisters, it dawned on me I should have bought some gloves. Still, what a feeling of accomplishment it was to see my paltry two metres of 'wall' manifest out of the earth, even if in retrospect it did look more like a rickety row of enamel-chipped teeth. It was baking, and I was drinking non-stop. I eyed the water tank again. Two litres down, twenty-eight to go.

I should point out here, there wasn't really much of a risk of me dying of thirst. My closest neighbour was four hundred metres away, and the handy public tap (of which there are so many in Turkey) was wedged eight hundred metres up a sharp slope in the graveyard. Still, unless I revolutionised the way I used water, things were going to get exceptionally inconvenient.

The sun had now shimmied behind the mountain signalling that afternoon was over and evening approaching. I tipped a little water from the tank into my hands to clean them, watching it trickle through my fingers and into the mud.

It was time to establish camp proper. I grabbed my new $50 Carrefour tent, and set about making what was to become my home for the next eight months. True, that tent changed positions more often than a mainstream politician. Even so, the bargain canvas far surpassed all expectations, and would survive well into the next year, until finally meeting its maker in a wrathful storm.

As the sky thickened with darkness, the distant lights from Alakır bay flicked on one by one. I realised I still hadn't eaten. By now I was almost staggering about in exhaustion having completed at least six or seven runs with the wheelbarrow, land terracing, camp founding and the like. The easiest thing I could think of preparing was a sandwich. There was more hand washing, then tomato washing. I ate, and drank. Made myself some tea. I was down to twenty-five litres with the washing-up now towering menacingly in the shadows. I was also filthy.

Night had well and truly fallen, and I was almost sleeping in my hiking boots. Dragging the plastic tankard of water next to the tent, I crouched and stuck my torch into it. I calculated I could spare about ten litres for a shower. Ten litres. It's a piffling amount, but that was all I had. I needed water for breakfast in the morning, and I didn't like the idea of completely running out. Turning around, I briefly caught the last outlines of the great pines that bordered the land disappearing into the pitch. I decided to forego my wash and sleep in my own grime.

As I pulled off my work clothes and lay on my new bed, how cosy it felt. The kilim on the floor was both warm and homely, the foam mattress as comfortable as any bed. I reached out for a last slug of water and wondered briefly how long I would manage to live up there like that. I wondered how long it would take me to get connected to the municipality supply too.

One and a half years on I still have no running water. And I've no longer any intention of getting any. An earthbag house has been built, tons of earth plaster made, plants planted, bathrooms erected and dismantled, animals fed, meals cooked, washing-up done. After that first night I think I managed to shower just about every day. You see, we humans are made of water, and water always finds a way. As I sit here in my earth covered roundhouse tapping away at my story, the winter rain is driving down. I can hear that deluge hammering on my roof and gurgling into the newly installed water storage tanks. I receive no bills. There's no direct debit. Water just comes. For free. As it always has and it always will.

But how have I managed until now? I've managed by being thrifty. Water really shouldn't be used just once, and there is a three-step system in operation in my kitchen.

Step 1: Clean water is used for washing vegetables. Step 2: Semi clean goes in the washing-up bowl. Step 3: Dirty water goes on the garden.

You need to be using bio-degradable detergent for such a program, but my basil plants thrived on the washing-up bowl throw-outs for more than eight months. In addition, I have a composting dry toilet, which abhors water, and I plant trees that are as thrifty as I am; olives, almonds, carobs, walnuts, and figs are highly sustainable in hot dry climates. Laundry was never the great problem I imagined it would be, as rocks and mountains care little about your wardrobe so you can wear the same thing until it stands up and walks away from you.

Water is the most important thing in the world. When it's no longer there that fact becomes very clear. It's insane how much we waste it, and pollute it and take this luscious resource for granted. So next time you leave the tap on, take a moment and spare a thought for me.

2013

Things that go Slither in the Night

January 2013

It was back in the beginning, May 2011, and the evenings were still cool. My silky blue dome was almost invisible, concealed within a circle of tall grass and thistles. It was my third night in the tent. Alone. In the dark. It was a darkness unlit by neon or streetlights, a pitch deep enough to devour entire mountains.

I woke up with a start. Something was slithering along the side of the canvas. Or was it scampering? It was hard to tell. I lay there unmoving, hardly daring to blink as I listened to the sinister rustling. I thought about the bag of sulphur I had forgotten to sprinkle along the circumference of my tent to ward off such unwanted guests. Balloons of fear began to swell inside me.

Tentatively, I slid my hand out to search for my torch. The noise continued. My imagination hurtled down a hundred dingy critter-filled alleys, tunnels brimming with poisonous vipers, scorpions the size of rats and other beasts of unknown ferocity just itching to chew holes in the groundsheet and eat me alive, or...or simply look ugly.

It took minutes of agonising fumbling, but I finally located the torch. I flicked it on. The squirming stopped. Hell! The beast was stalking me.

After fear, the next pit-stop on survival's race track is aggression. By now I was wide awake, sitting bolt upright with more than a sensible amount of adrenalin careering through my system. Realising sleep was out of the question, I decided I'd rather be the hunter than the hunted.

As slowly and quietly as I could, I unzipped the mosquito net door, dementedly flashing the torch this way and that like a cop in a bad movie. Still no noise. Whatever it was, was hiding. So out I crept. I stood up, running the beam frantically over the canvas. And then I saw it. The perpetrator of my insomnia. The heinous leviathan of my nightmares...a lizard. Tiny, web-footed, rather sweet. The small reptile peered up at me petrified, beady lizard eyes popping. I exhaled, feeling idiotic. Lizard and I stared at each other for a moment or two before I crouched back into the tent. As I lay back down on my sleeping bag, I mused how, despite not having owned a television for the last fifteen years, I had nonetheless become yet another victim of Hollywood's relentless fear-mongering.

There is an entire industry founded on generating fear of wildlife. Horror films have been quick to cash in on the myriad of unusual fauna in the world. *Anaconda*, *The Birds*, and *Jaws* are but a few of the animal-based movies that spring to mind. Pretty much any creature that has the misfortune to crawl, slide or not possess fur is subject to a bizarre kind of demonization. The result is, when we're left to our own devices out in the wild, especially at night, those monster movie images take on a life of their own. They make us paranoid and consequently aggressive to all around.

The morning after 'lizard night', I stepped out of my tent and stumbled into my make-shift 'kitchen'. In truth it was more of a food area, with a ramshackle washing-up stand cobbled together from broken sticks.

(Oh the many benefits of Girl Guides.) But I was struck by something else. I realised as I looked about that there were no crumbs anywhere, no left-overs to clean up. In short, no mess at all. Hmm, had this been what my nocturnal guest had been after?

From then on, I took time to venture out of my tent in the dark hours and observe what was actually occurring in the big bad pitch beyond my canvas. It was fantastic. What I saw was a carefully timed banquet. First to arrive were the cats. They rooted through my bin and polished off the larger scraps. Next, the field mice crept by. Finally, there were parties of lizards, skinks and agamas that cleaned up the crumbs. There was a tawny owl too. It came most nights, calling into the darkness to its mate down in the valley, before presumably hunting down one or two unsuspecting reptiles.

But it was a month later that something really dragged me to my senses. Every morning I would open up a large *kilim* onto the bare earth for my morning yoga practice. Once I was done, I had to fold the carpet up quickly, otherwise the late spring wind blew burrs that would enmesh themselves in the weave. One day, I forgot to fold up the rug. I came back in the evening to see it covered in thistles and spiky caterpillar-like burrs. I groaned. They could only be removed one by one. It was a laborious, finger scratching process. The upshot was, I couldn't be bothered, so I left it. The next morning when I chanced to walk by the rug, what should I see? Ants. Hundreds of them. They had turned my yoga carpet into an insect spaghetti junction. Agh! Then something caught my eye. I noticed two of the ants tugging at a burr, and another carrying one off.

As it happened, I'd just finished reading a book about humanity's special relationship to their own land, or domain. I think if I hadn't actually been living in the wild it would have written the work off as nonsense. One of the things the book stated was that when a human owns a domain and loves it, all the wildlife within the area will begin to support them. I regarded the traffic of ants streaming across my *kilim*. I rubbed my chin, scratched my head, and turned around. Next day I left for the beach.

When I returned in the evening I couldn't believe my eyes. My rug was spotless. Completely and utterly. It looked as though it had been picked clean by a school of tweezer-brandishing elves. I began to look at animals in a vastly different light. I have become very humbled by them to be honest. Because all of them, even the scaliest, slimiest or most arthropod, are incredibly benign. In fact they are not only harmless, they are invaluable, helpful little mates (when treated appropriately). My kitchen is a case in point. Whilst it has bloomed in size, and enjoyed multiple locations, it remains completely open. I never sweep it or wash the floor. I leave my used saucepans out at night as well. Every morning I wake to find my band of nocturnal helpers has cleaned up the lot.

Thus the bag of sulphur I had bought for protection was never opened. Suddenly, I didn't want to harm anything and I believed, rightly or wrongly, that nothing would harm me in return. Perhaps it was coincidence. Perhaps I was just lucky. I lived outside in the wild for the duration of eight months, and the only snake I ever saw was a tiny grass snake on the border. No wild boar entered the land either. My pomegranate growing neighbours (boar love pomegranates) believed they were warded off by the smell of a human sleeping outside. There were no spider bites, no scorpion stings, no Ottoman vipers found lurking in the toilet. It was almost as though the land was blessed.

My gardener owns an enormous Anatolian shepherd called Apo. He's the size a small lion. Apo took to the domain so much he began a protective nightly watch. Sitting by his side, I would run my hands through his thick fur and marvel how such a huge carnivorous animal could be so gentle. Together we would stare out over a starlit valley listening to the tawny owl hoot overhead and the agamas scampering below. I began to feel that this might just be what paradise is like.

Power Revolution

February 2013

"So you can't watch any television up there?"

I shook my head. My cousin Jeanette tugged at her bangs and sat back in her armchair. We were far from the hills of Turkey now, snuggled in my aunt's home in deepest, darkest Norfolk.

"But, I do have the internet. There's a great little USB device I can use in Turkey. As long as my computer's charged I can connect pretty much anywhere."

Jeanette grinned. "Internet in a tent? That's hilarious." Then she picked up her coffee cup. "But I could never live like that, I mean no electricity. It's great, I love hearing about it, but I'd never do it."

From the distant place her eyes rolled to, I gauged she was imagining the implications of my life in all its powerless, waterless glory. And from the look on her face the implications weren't good. My ninety-four-year-old gran was huddled in the leather sofa next to us, ears straining to follow the conversation. She screwed up her brow on her beautiful (and yes my gran is still beautiful) face.

"Did you say you have internet in your tent?" she said. Gran's eyes – eyes that have seen the birth of television, a world war, the Berlin Wall go up and then down, and the techno-revolution – wrinkled in disbelief. She crossed one leg daintily over the other and folded her hands in her lap. "Well, I never did!" she said. "I couldn't fathom it even in a house. But a tent!" From the way her face crumpled we gathered she was caught somewhere between amazement and dismay. "Ooh," she shuddered, "It's all beyond me."

We all laughed. The light was already dying in the room, so my aunt reached over and flicked on the lamp. The hedgerow outside faded out of sight. Suddenly Jeanette pulled herself upright. Her eyes widened like a pair of Liquorice Allsorts. She opened her mouth.

"Oh my God!" We all turned in her direction. She was staring at me, appalled. "You mean you can't use *hair straighteners?*"

Back in the Carrefour tent on the dry summer hills of a Turkish village, I woke up. The sun had just crawled over the first mountain peak. From my bed I could see the slopes bathed in the rosy glow of fresh morning. The birds were chirping in such a state of excitement, it was infectious. I had no alarm clock wrecking my slumber, no job to get up for. It was still not even six am. Yet I sprang out of that bed like a hare with a pin in its backside. I didn't want to miss those early morning hours. They are sublime.

As life goes by I realise just how gifted humans are. We are adaptable beyond belief. Yesterday's inconceivable nightmare becomes tomorrow's reality. All realities have their pros and cons. I was without power which had its limitations. But a new life was unfolding. And the fact was I loved it.

I'd been on the land about three months by then, and something of a routine had emerged. As soon as I had stepped out of my tent, I stretched, and walked about my domain. It was the beginning of July, and those early hours were pleasantly cool. The plants gleamed as the first rays of sunlight hit them and everything on the land began rushing about its business before the heat of the day set in. There were no rough man-made noises. No cars, no machines. Instead I was wandering within a symphony composed by nature. It made me feel happy and alive.

After my walk I would do some yoga, followed by a bit of meditation. Next I'd prepare myself a nice, big Turkish breakfast; eggs, salad, olives, cheese, bread, honey, fried peppers and potatoes, all washed down with a pot of coffee. The day would by now have rolled on. The land would be buckling up for some serious sun. As I swung in the hammock, I would look about my campsite and wonder what today's project would be. Should I start the tool shed? Or paint some stones to sell? When it got too hot I would drive to the sea for a swim. Thus my days unwound.

I have to be honest, I wasn't missing hair straighteners. Nor television. The view from my land was so inspiring and the wildlife so varied I felt constantly entertained. I was also locked into a pyramid of need in which electricity was the least of my worries. Water was always my number one headache. However, there was one issue related to power that changed my life. Night time. Without power you're well and truly in the dark. True, there are torches, and candles, but it's still difficult to cook, read or have any sort of nightlife without decent lighting.

Very quickly my days morphed into new shapes. I switched from late nights and leisurely awakenings, to early rises and early sleeps. Unwittingly I fell into what Chinese medicine would call the ideal sleep cycle. Our bodies are designed to wake up with the sun. Our internal organs rest and clean themselves in the dark hours. When we don't respect this natural rhythm, we become sick or depressed or both. By July I could feel the difference. The lack of electricity had inadvertently done me an enormous favour.

Now eighteen months later, it pays for me to remember this. Because there has been a revolution on my land. Last week I installed solar power. It's incredible. For the first time in nearly two years I have light, I have sound, I have a jig-saw. And most importantly I have a computer that I don't need to run up the hill to my neighbour every day to charge. This is all fantastic. But before I rush to buy speakers, or begin a twelve-hour electric sanding campaign, I'm pausing a little. I can hear the noise of the wind rushing through the great pines, a robin is twittering in one of the olive trees, the plants are rocking in the air, waving to me to get off my computer and touch them. When I pull back from my laptop screen I see from my window the mountains cascading into Alakır bay. The creases in their slopes dance as the sun moves over the sky. It's never the same dance. Blink and you've missed it.

Yes I need to remember this. It pays to go slow. From one day to the next I've gone from zero power to being inundated with electricity. Yet I have learned something important these past two years, and it's nothing to do with survival. What I've learned is this: convenience doesn't necessarily make you happy. And there's more to life than just being comfortable.

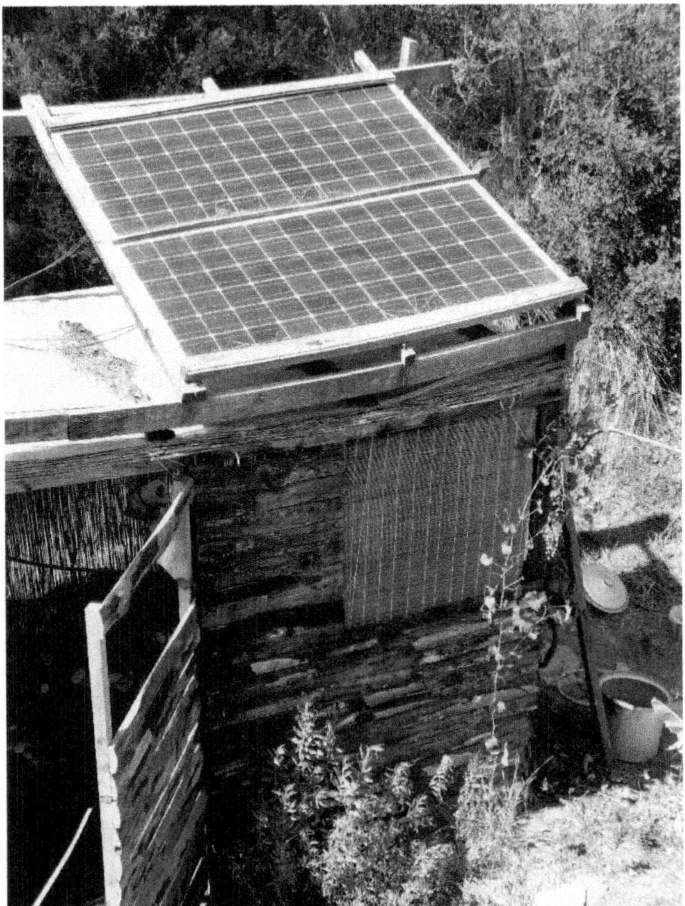

Building for Beginners

March 2013

How does anyone go from not being able to bang a nail in, without either bending it or smacking a finger, to constructing a house, in the space of six months?

The answer lies far from building manuals, workshops, and training. It resides a long way from the Turkish mountains too. But first, let me rewind to the beginning of my building adventure. The first month on my land. Just one woman, a tent, and a dubious stick creation that paraded under the term 'washing-up rack'.

The month of May was gobbling up its days like they were baklava. Syrupy, sweet days they were too, with clear skies of cobalt, and mountain outlines sharp enough to cleave the unblemished blue into bite-sized triangles. The green slopes that rolled and swirled about me were on the brink of yellowing, late spring flowers itching to scatter their seeds. It was with this backdrop that I embarked on my first construction project; the toilet.

There were always plenty of questions about my lifestyle. But it was in particular my bathroom habits that seemed to ignite people's curiosity. Where did I crap? How did I wash? After a couple of weeks of answering nature's many calls in various 'off-land' locations, I accepted that some sort of bathroom was imperative. Thus I made one...in a manner of speaking. As with every new step I took up there on my mountain,

I looked to the land to show me the way first. Was there a spot that nature had divined would be my WC?

I found a small rock-strewn cove at the edge of the forest. It was surrounded by wild shrubs and trees. Thorn bushes scratched at the gaps with their thick green claws. Pushing through an olive tree, I edged into the space within. I was almost invisible to the outside world. Despite its seclusion, the clearing looked out onto the pomegranate fields beyond. A loo with a view? Ha ha! It seemed my bathroom space had made itself known. But how to go about constructing it? It was then that I drew on the only building experience I possessed; den building. I had to dig quite far into my memory to locate those indispensable life lessons. The last time I had made a den, I'd been seven or eight years old at most.

I don't know if all children build dens, but I think most of the kids on my street did. There were bed sheet hideouts, shelters woven from branches, and my favourite was a moss-carpeted kitchen I made with a girl called Isabelle Dobby. We crafted it under a knotty old tree near her house using the gaps in the roots as cupboards and shelves. Yes, indeed. A moss carpet. It was state-of-the-art in the den world, even if I say so myself.

Back in Turkey, well over thirty years on, this was all coming back to me. As I examined the circle of greenery at the edge of the forest that was bidding to be my bathroom, I looked at it as a child might. I studied the shape of the rocks, the placement of grasses, the spaces. Then I rolled up my sleeves and set about the brambly little circle. Oh what happy hours I spent that day, clearing a showering area, collecting small stones to spread on the floor to stop the ground becoming muddy, inventing a neat little canister-with-hose-shower. But it was the bathroom 'door' that was my pride and joy. I found two sturdy sticks, buried them in the ground, searched out a third branch that arced beautifully and rested it over the other two sticks. Then...wait for it...*I nailed them together*. This may seem like rather a piffling achievement to other more experienced artisans, but for me it was the first thing I'd ever nailed in my life. Voila! A doorway appeared. I found an old curtain and pegged it over the top (den-building tactics revisited) and that was that.

It might seem that I'm over simplifying, but that bathroom 'door' was a turning point. It was the baby step that empowered me to move on from toilet to tool shed to wooden deck to house, all in the space of half a year. Each time it was the same process. Look at the land, look at what you have, use some logic and just try it out.

About two months later, one of my neighbour's relatives turned up to take a look about my homemade kingdom on the hill. She tucked a grey, silken headscarf around her head and wobbled as she walked the length of the track. On arriving before the toilet, she tweaked the curtain and peered inside. Next, she looked at my tent and my kitchen, with its tree branch hooks and random wood slats for shelving. She turned up her nose.

"Ooh, I don't like it at all. It's...it's like a kid's game or something. Why don't you make a *proper* house?"

She was right. It was just like a kid's game. And that's exactly what made the entire adventure so much fun, and ultimately possible at all.

Now, two years on, I'm sitting in a roundhouse made of mud. My kitchen is a rubble-filled mess. There are stray stones everywhere, and my sink seems to change places every day. There are still gaps all over the walls where I need to finish the earth plaster. The windowsills are not yet installed, nor do I have any furniture. I sleep on the floor in a sleeping bag, like a child in a backyard. Does the chaos drive me crackers? No. Strangely, it doesn't. Because it's a game. A big, muddy game. And I love every single minute of it.

The Hairy Green Approach to Well-Being

April 2013

One summer morning back in 2011 something significant happened. The sun had turned into a blazing white ogre. It had a pelt of fire and a stare that could fry the skin clean off a capsicum. It was the end of July. And July on the southern coast is when folk run for shade, or water, or air-conditioned malls. Nothing can survive in that heat. Grass withers. Mammals flop dejectedly under trees. Even the great pines, some at least a hundred years old, no longer stretch for the heavens. Their stance becomes one of stoic endurance as a lifeless dust slowly coats their branches.

This wasn't in itself significant, however. Summer happens every year. Granted, we always forget. From the lamenting every July you'd be forgiven for thinking it was the first summer to ever see the wrong side of forty degrees. Streets empty, people flake out in gazebos. Sometimes they refuse to get out of bed at all.

"*Çoook sıcak yaaa!*" (It's sooo hot!) they wail before they drop back and reach for an ice cream.

But that July, the July of 2011, I wasn't one of those late risers. I had to be out of my tent by seven. It was no longer because I was bounding with enthusiasm vis-à-vis any number of construction projects, nor was it eagerness to watch the pink wave of dawn roll over the mountain peaks. I had to be out, because being 'in' was tantamount to wrapping yourself in cellophane and bedding down in a Turkish bath.

I reached forward and pulled myself out of the canvas. Immediately I winced and grabbed back my hand. I'd branded myself on one of the tent pegs that had the misfortune of being in the sun's path. Finally I stood up and surveyed my queendom. It was a sorry sight, a rolling slope of yellowing expiration. The top terrace of the land, where my tent was pitched, was even worse. It was south Turkey's answer to the Gobi. Cracks zigzagged through the waterless earth. And where there were no cracks there was dust.

I turned to head for the 'kitchen'. It was then that I noticed it. The significant thing. There, a little in front of the tent, was a small patch of green.

I blinked. No. Nothing could ever grow independently on this broiling plateau of death. It was impossible. I moved towards the mysterious green entity in disbelief. There before my eyes a plant was sprouting. Seeing is believing, they say. Well sometimes it's the other way round. Now I believed, and thus I saw. As I picked my way through my desert, I found tens of these plants. Where had they come from? It was as though they'd been waiting all summer for everything to collapse, before they raised their hairy little arms and shouted, 'Ha ha! Our turn now.'

I had read somewhere when you love your domain and set the intention for it to be yours, everything within it tilts towards you. I was gradually becoming something of a natural magic apostle. The land itself was my balm. The animals my affection. What about the vegetation though? Was there a reason this strange little plant had popped up? Should I make a tea out of it? Was it medicinal? Hallucinogenic even?

The days went by and the peculiar heat-spurning plants grew. They weren't particularly attractive, a little like rosemary but floppier and messier, which was unfortunate. I can become obsessed with aesthetics at times. The plant was ugly, so I began to ignore it. I think I might have even called it a weed.

Then one day I noticed this 'weed' cluttering about a tiny grape-vine remnant I was trying to salvage. At some point in the past either a person or a bird must have dropped a grape seed. The seed had struggled. It had sprouted. Now, in midsummer a few feeble cricket-eaten leaves were hanging desperately onto existence. Every now and again I'd throw my washing-up water over them and try and talk the baby vine into surviving. Now here was this opportunistic weed cashing in and usurping the moisture! Grrr. I stormed towards the prolific newcomer with intent.

Ha! In one quick snatch I'd uprooted it. I threw it to one side. Or rather I tried to throw it, because it was sticky, as if secreting oil. Pausing a little, I noticed a smell. It was a cross between lavender and eucalyptus. I took a deep breath. The aroma was out of this world! I found the fragrance so refreshing I began to use it for washing in, a sort of natural aromatherapy. When I did I was swept away by the cooling sense of well-being it bathed me in.

As the summer deepened, our village became steeped in such high temperatures we all developed heat rashes. Our legs itched. Our arms itched. And the hotter it got, the more red spots appeared. I washed in my weed-water. My rash vanished.

Soon enough the sun began to shed its monstrous summer bulk. As it slimmed it dropped lower in the sky. The days drew in. My herb receded back into the earth. I never learned its name. No one around here seemed to know. 'Smelly weed' was the best anyone could do.

Since then all sorts of other natural growth has come to my attention. I have only a couple of acres of land but it's a living, breathing apothecary. Some of it is edible, some drinkable. Some plants heal ailments, others nourish, some are so beautiful to look at you can't help but feel inspired. There are gels and fragrances and poultices, berries and potpourri, colour therapy, pollen and herbs. Each month the selection changes, as do my needs. We are all, from the earth, to the plants to the animals, moving in sync.

This rediscovery of what at one time must have been common knowledge is enthralling. I've merely stroked the grassy surface of my wonderland. Even so, I'm sensing well-being isn't something we have to struggle for years to earn. It's our birthright. It's where we come from. All we have to do is go home, live there and notice it.

The Builder's Road to Enlightenment

May 2013

Ten days ago I hurt my knee. It's a recurring injury exacerbated by car driving. The repetitive tension while pressing the gas pedal has caused inflammation of my knee tendons. Hmm. Am I the only one seeing the metaphor?

Being the obstinate sort that I am, it's taken a while for me to accept that I might need to slow down a little. I really don't want to. I have so many plans and ideas, and I'm itching to bring them to fruition. No chance right now. My knee has given up the ghost, temporarily at least.

So, with all this immobility, there has been time on my hands for a little reflection.

A few mornings ago, I decided to stretch my ailing leg. Stepping onto my wooden platform, I struck a few yoga poses. I inhaled the clear, late-spring air. Looking over the yellowing hill, a slope that was as verdant as a rainforest a month ago, I was reminded of how quickly things change. This plot of land, the valley, in fact our entire worlds are perpetually dynamic pictures.

As I finished my yoga session and lay in relaxation, I heard a flurry of activity from the pine tree next to my kitchen. A swirl of bee-eater birds rose like a plume of electric blue smoke. The cloud pulsed in the air. It resembled a genie, inhaling and exhaling.

Bee-eater birds migrate from Africa in late spring. As their name suggests they munch on bees. My village holds a huddle of bee-keepers, which is why these attractive and vividly-marked birds grace us with their presence. Naturally, bee-keepers and bee-eaters are not the best of friends, and the locals will routinely pull a shot gun out whenever they see a bee-eater swarm in the vicinity. Seeing as both bees and bee-eaters are dwindling in numbers I'm ambivalent about the ethics of that. But I'm not of the shooting disposition, thus the bee-eaters choose my pines to overnight in.

That morning, as I lay on the platform post-yoga and stared into the sky, I was mesmerised by the bee-eaters. They circled and dove directly above me, creating a living, moving display of such beauty and precision it was almost hard to believe it hadn't been choreographed for the purpose.

My mind returned to my knee and the gas pedal, to driving at break-neck speed after goals, to all the grand plans of my life, none of which have ever turned out how I thought. This adventure, the mountain-house adventure, is an anomaly in my life. It was never planned for. It was never on my 'to-do' list at all. I had no great vision of building my own home because I had never considered such a thing could ever give me so much pleasure. But this space apparently didn't need a plan. It was almost as if it grew by itself, a little like the wild grapevine next to my toilet.

Before this home, I thought I had to do yoga, to breathe and meditate, and follow a set path, in order to find peace and happiness. I was driven, hot on the trail of the elusive goal of enlightenment that so many people bang on about. But awakening is everywhere. It surfs along the sunlight that illuminates the leaves, it flirts with the movement of the air, it thrives in the plants bursting through the soil. It lives in us too.

It's all quite peculiar really. My bank balance is fairly pathetic. I have no romantic relationship, no prestigious job, no luxury car. In fact I have none of the things the powers-that-be would have us believe we need for success or happiness. None of this matters one iota, because however it appears on the outside, on the inside I feel overwhelmingly complete, almost as though I've made it.

I think life is like the bee-eaters. It swirls and dances and makes us gasp in wonder. Things appear and disappear in their own time. Often when we look back over our shoulders, we haven't a clue how it all came to be. It's almost as if it just 'happened'.

Even so, every now and again I'll still kid myself into believing there are things I have to do. I'll look life in the eye and issue it a few ultimatums, things like, 'the kitchen *must* be finished by next month', or 'we're going to get that plaster on, what*ever* it takes'.

And life looks at me, nods ironically and grins. 'Really?' it says. 'You think so?' Then it'll give me a knee injury. Or send a deluge of rain. Or make my car break down. Because the picture of our lives can't be forced or mapped, or even perhaps imagined. We are both creators and creations simultaneously.

I still do yoga and meditate. I still drive too fast as well. But honestly, it was participating in the creation of my home – a home that listened to the Earth – that was ultimately the most enlightening.

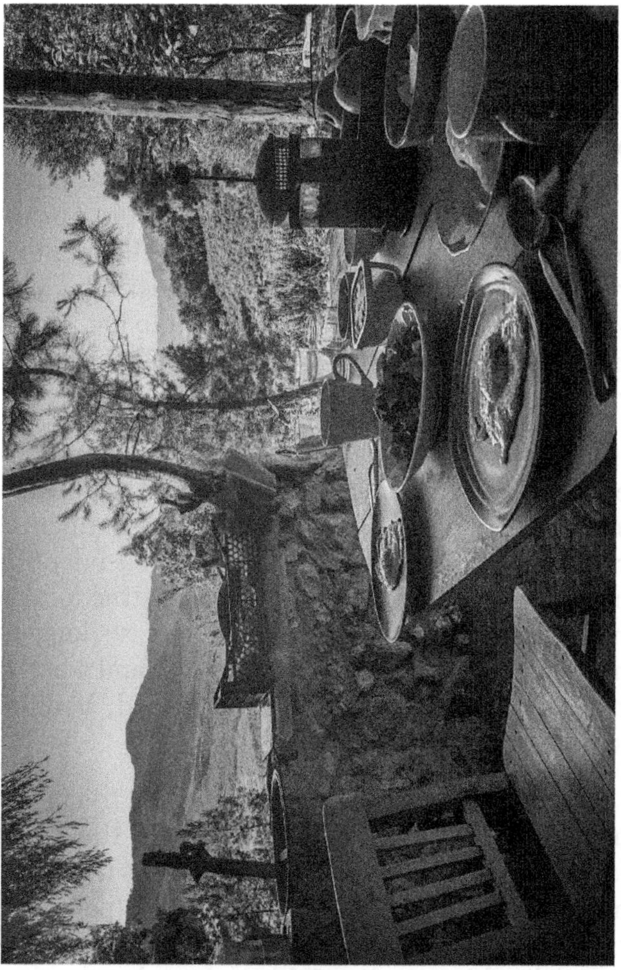

Creating Worlds

June 2013

How optimistic we were ten days ago. Gezi Park in Istanbul was a space bubbling with kids painting murals, melodies streamed from the fingers of a world class pianist playing day and night, people had constructed a communal library, the peaceful protest/festival was encircled by a chain of well-wishing mothers. It was all quite wonderfully idealist. A tiny vision of a better world brought to life. Then the police stormed in with the tear gas and the chemical water, and the vision – it seemed – was shattered.

When I saw the images of panic rolling through my feed last Sunday and Monday, I was momentarily knocked off balance. There was disappointment and frustration. How could such a well-intentioned movement be subject to so much destruction? And then I remembered another time not so long back that I'd felt the same way. It was a year and a half ago. It was winter. I was knee-deep in mud, building a home.

Back in late December 2011, I was still trying, albeit unsuccessfully, to live in a tent. By then the earthbag house was essentially up and the roof was on. Only the mud plaster remained. In fact, at that point I was reeling at just how quickly a vision of a home had materialised into reality. I felt supremely empowered. But winter was roaring towards me, unleashing its volley of floods and hurricanes. As we began to stomp the plaster I realised I was tired. I was feeling like a refugee wandering from neighbour to neighbour in a bid to escape the cold and the wet. I needed a home and a rest.

Desperately, hurriedly, the earthbag team and I applied our earth plaster to the walls. Once the house was covered, we waited for it to dry. My shelter, my new life, would soon be complete. Or so I thought. While the plaster hardened, I flew to England for Christmas. I quite expected to return to my earthbag house two weeks later and unpack my suitcases. Unfortunately, that wasn't how it turned out.

I remember the day of my return vividly. I unloaded my bags from the car and then picked my way through the squelching mud. The house loomed before me. On seeing the plaster, my heart nearly stopped beating. Everywhere enormous cracks zigzagged along the mud walls. It looked like a circular Arizona.

Dropping the bags, I ran up to the walls and walked around them. The cracks were great gashes. In places the plaster had simply fallen off. It was so ugly and demonstrably unsound, the house would clearly have to be entirely replastered. That would take weeks. Meanwhile I was homeless. I was also now clean out of money.

I slumped on a rock and stared glumly at what should have been my new world, but wasn't. I wondered what to do. Shivering in the cold winter air, I pulled out my phone. I called the only person who knew anything about earthbagging in Turkey at the time, the person who had inspired me in the first place; my friend Chris, who had built a string of earthbag bungalows in the Kabak valley. The sky blanched above me. A branch from the olive tree in front of me bowed in the wind. The phone picked up.

How miserable I felt as I relayed the state of my plaster. I was very much on the brink of tears.

"Ah don't be disappointed," said the voice of experience on the other end. "It's all part of the creation process. You'll find a solution."

That moment is a poignant one for me. The moment of sitting on the rock and hearing my disappointment echoed back at me. Because I *was* feeling inordinately disappointed. In my mind's eye it was as if the plaster cracks had destroyed my entire house. My vision was ruined. And that's how I felt when I saw the destruction of Gezi Park too.

So what happened with my earth plaster in the end?

Because I had run out of money, and because I needed a place to lay my head and take a shower, I chose to return to Taiwan and teach for six months (though there was a fair amount of hand-wringing in between). Ultimately it was a good thing. I rested physically. I regrouped. Then I came back in September with money in my pocket and energy in my muscles.

The most striking part of the episode was that of all the earthbag construction skills I learned over the past two years, it's the earth plaster that has become my ultimate creation. Nine months ago Celal and I set about engineering a new invincible master batch of the mix. We slowly and deliberately tested different concoctions. I made more mistakes. Lumps appeared on the walls. To hide them, I began to sculpt the plaster. A tree manifested out of the mud. Then another. Then stone walls, shelves, mosaics.

I now take inspiration from those times of earthbag chaos, because I see how much my muddy roundhouse creation, with all its slips and slides and messiness, aptly reflects what Turkey is currently experiencing. After all, the Turkish Tree Revolution has grown out of a vision of a more beautiful, more equal, freer world. It is a creation in the making, just like my home.

But that home took time to construct. And it wasn't all a bowl of earth cherries. Sometimes it was a large disintegrating circle of mud.

So while we, the people of Turkey, may feel disappointment at not being heard, while we may feel frustration at our vision for a freer, more democratic Turkey being stopped in its tracks, it pays to remember. Visions are seeds, and as such can never be shattered. Their growth is merely stalled for a while, and that incubation period I have learned is crucial. It's a time to regroup and re-evaluate, a time to perfect the creation.

At times the images from the streets are evocative, at times inspiring, and at other times – such as now – profoundly disturbing. It is the 25th day of the Turkish Tree Revolution, a movement that has soared and plunged and stretched its branches along the full extent of the emotional spectrum. The seed vision has begun to manifest into a sapling of reality. That small tree may be losing a few leaves as it finds its footing on the Earth. But it is still very much alive, and it's consolidating its power. Who can say in the end what it will become? But step by step, day by day, it's growing.

I hope to look back on this moment in Turkish history in the same way I look back at the loaded moment I was sitting so disheartened on a rock, calling for help. A moment that I misconstrued as going wrong, but was in fact the crux of an invincible, original creation.

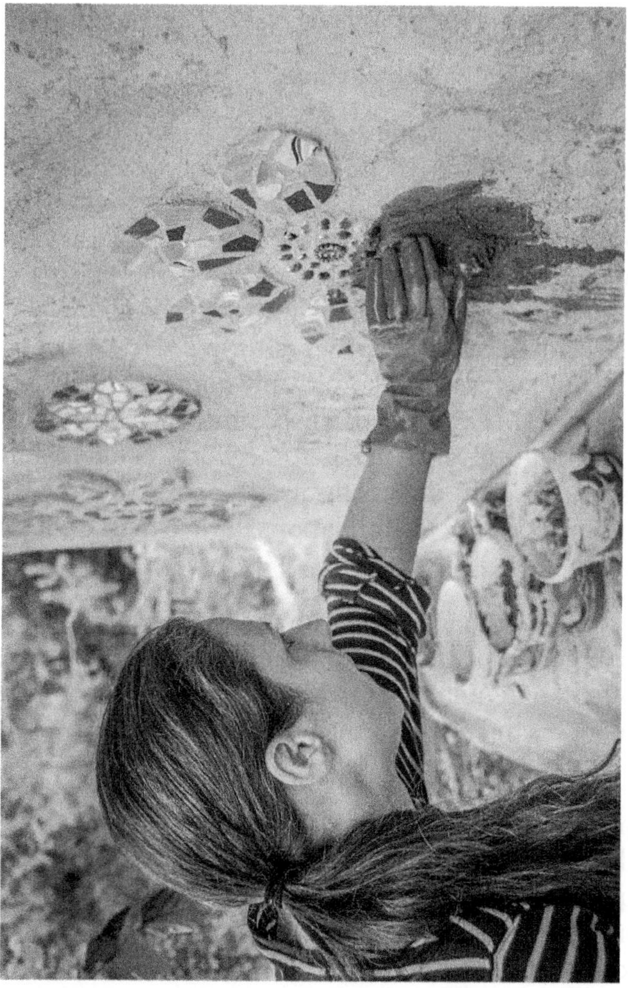

Loneliness

July 2013

"Don't you get lonely up here?"

It has to be the question I hear most often whenever someone is intrepid enough to pay me a visit. True, that question might take a while to form. The journey to my home is a process after all. Tongues loll out as friends hike down the sun-broiled track. At the bottom they spot my earth roof, and my water tank skulking behind the undergrowth. A corner is turned. Hearts probably sink as my guests step past my compost heap on the right, and the tower of dusty lime bags on the left. I admit the entrance needs some work. Finally the land is reached. The view rolls away from the visitors. It's a fir-speckled rug of undulations unravelling down to the sea.

My earthbag house now looms; a circle of dirt poking out of the land like an upturned hat. There is often some analogy to the Smurfs at this point, and more pertinently to Smurfette.

My visitors take a peek inside. They imbibe the earth plaster sculptures, and again the view framed in the doorway. They become quiet. My land has a habit of quieting people, I've noticed that. The key is turned in imaginations, and visions move into gear. I think I know what my friends are thinking. *Could I do this? Would I want to do this? And if I did this, what would I do differently?*

Sooner or later the question pops out. "Don't you get lonely up here?"

And I don't know how to answer it, because the answer I give always sounds trite. No. I *never* feel lonely. This isn't because I'm a freak, nor a Buddha, nor even Smurfette. I've felt lonely many times in my life; lonely in crowds, lonely at parties, lonely when I didn't fit in, and loneliest of all in romantic relationships. But it's difficult to explain why there's no loneliness here in the mountains, unless you experience it. I think loneliness is the sensation of not being accepted for who you are. It is also a feeling of disconnectedness, of not fitting in. And here, snuggled in the arms of pure nature, where the judgments of other humans are inaudible, I am accepted. I am whole. I fit in.

I am also never alone. It might look as though I'm alone, if you think aloneness is merely the absence of other human beings. But I'm not. I've become very clear about that over the last two years. The land and every living entity in it communes with me. It is obvious. Yet only if you are quiet. And only if you meet it halfway. People scoff at the idea of plants and insects possessing any kind of sophisticated sentience. I would certainly agree that it's a self-fulfilling prophecy. So you can choose. Either you see life and love in all things, or you don't. Either you reach out to the trees and the lizards, and let them speak to you, or you focus blindly on humanity as the only source of intelligence and filter your ability to connect accordingly. It's a free world. It's a choice.

When you do give nature a chance, when you ratchet up the sensitivity dial inside you and tune in, magic blooms. Vegetable plants burgeon before your eyes, trees pour energy into you, vipers leave you alone, and camel spiders begin to look charming. Whether it's pheromones, energy fields or some sort of shared consciousness, I have no idea. I only know that attitude is everything. The moment you treat any living being with respect, when you consider it as your partner or friend or equal, when you genuinely care for it, that being transforms. Conversely when you mock, abuse, fear or disregard the same thing, it disengages from you or attacks you.

So when the sun sinks a little lower behind the great pines, and the coffee pot is empty, my visitors make their way up the track and back to the world out there. As dusk rises and does away with the shadows, the plants begin to glow. It's an ensorcelling colour green they emit at that hour, a light that evokes Narnias and Secret Gardens. I begin my watering ritual. As my vegetable patch shudders under my simulation of rain, I feel a sense of connection and well-being I rarely experience with people. It seems to radiate through the pores in my skin and fill up the entire garden. This land is a part of me, and I'm a part of it. This has made me understand my place on the planet too, a place of connected participation.

I see the first street lamp pierce the evening down in Alakır bay. I imagine the prattle and the gossip down there, the noise of humans and their desperate clamour for attention, the competitiveness, the condemnations hidden in the creases of smiles, the obsessive need to be right, the disguised slights, the guilt-tripping, the empty talk about nothing. Perhaps not all human interaction is quite this negative, but when you pull the façade off most conversations, how many are really based on mutual respect, kindness and caring? How many make you feel truly fulfilled?

Then it's my turn to ask. I whisper into the wind, and let it carry my words all the way over to the lights at sea-level. "Don't you get lonely down there?"

The Luxury of Being Skint

August 2013

I'm skint, and I have been for about four years. It wasn't always this way. Before 2009 I was flush. I waltzed about the city of Antalya throwing money left, right and centre like confetti. I nibbled on absurdly priced pastries in top-notch restaurants, and terrorized the streets of Turkey in a spanking new Toyota Yaris. Oh it was the high life and I wouldn't deny it, I loved it.

And then, as often happens in life, one day it all disappeared. How it disappeared is not the issue. We are usually curious about downturns in other people's luck because we think if we uncover the 'mistake' the other made, we can safeguard ourselves from the same fate. But safeguarding isn't the point here. Because what we're so often safeguarding against is the best thing that could happen to us. So I'll say it again. I was prosperous before. It was fun. Now I'm skint. And do you know what? It's better than being flush.

Skint is a fantastic word, often to be heard scudding through the dulcet vowel tones of my native Essex vernacular. It's a variant of 'skinned', referring to the condition of not having money, and it is precise in its meaning. This meaning is important, because skint is not poor. Though you'd think, from the way we have been educated, that moneylessness and poverty were one and the same thing.

Poverty is a scourge that has little to do with your bank balance. There is cultural poverty, emotional poverty, material poverty, intellectual poverty and perhaps most detrimental of all, poverty of the imagination. It's a state of privation and a mindset of neediness, dark and thwarting in its suffocation.

Losing money made me realise that I could never really be poor, for the simple fact I am already inherently rich. We all are. The idea that we desperately need money has created a deep poverty of spirit, and the advertising industry, with its empty obsessions, has turned our imaginations and self-confidence to slush.

I live on about £200 a month, which I earn from my writing. I have no car, no iPhone, no Dolce & Gabbana handbag. I live in a mud hut up a mountain. Well...only when it rains. Apart from that I sleep under the stars, and recline on second-hand armchairs in the forest. This isn't a stance of moral or ecological one-upmanship. It's a preference. It's true I have worked for money, and that money has bought me my land. But by peeling away the layers and layers of the unnecessary, I have somehow, almost inadvertently stumbled into the life of my dreams. I no longer experience the lurching dread of Monday mornings. There is no 7 am panic. I take an hour or more to eat breakfast. I have no boss.

Now let me get it straight. I'm not judging all that money can buy as bad. And to have no money at all, or to be deprived of the basic resources is a desperate state of affairs. But let's be honest, those necessities are things like clean water, air, food and shelter, not a car or a new pair of shoes. Not that I'm exhorting the world to suddenly give up their cars. I've spent years loving driving and only sold mine last month. I'm merely pointing out, the car is a preference, not a need. The moment you no longer have one, that becomes obvious.

Money, when it works, is a useful exchange system (though there are others that are fairer and don't involve banks), and there is a certain pleasure to be derived from some of the merchandise it can procure. Even so, money is not all that it's cracked up to be, and acquiring the stuff can prove far more painful than the experience of living without it. Which brings me back to why I actually prefer being skint. Because I've woken up (a little late some might say) to the severely unadvertised fact that there are many things that only moneylessness can buy.

So, just for the record, here it is; a list of some of the benefits of being wonderfully, gloriously, luxuriously skint:

1. You tend not to get ripped off when you're skint. Fraudsters know you're an empty vessel, so they steer well clear. Burglars are apathetic as well. You can leave your door unlocked, because there's nothing to lock up.

2. You soon learn who your friends are. And believe me you *do* have friends who like you for more than what they can squeeze out of you. It's comforting to know you are worth more than your status symbols and the 'prestige' of your career.

3. You have nothing to lose. That's liberating.

4. You become extremely creative as your imagination starts to burn on all thrusters.

5. You stop throwing things away. This is both good for your soul and the environment.

6. You make 'downgrades' which often prove to be upgrades. I sold my car and bought a motorbike

instead. I cannot tell you how much I love the feel of the wind in my hair as I roar along the country lanes.

7. You engage in bank free, money free exchanges. I scuba dive as often as I want all summer long thanks to an exchange deal with my local dive centre. Everybody wins. They get a free helping hand for the busiest three weeks of the year and I get free dives.

8. You slow down and watch the flowers grow. Money and earning it often seems to involve a lot of haste. Things take longer without heaps of cash, but who cares? It's not a race, is it?

9. The best bit about being skint is that soon enough you learn to live on very little, which means you no longer have to work all the hours to 'survive'. With all that free time you can explore any number of hobbies that don't require money, things like: creating your own blog and waffling to your heart's content on it, tree climbing, philosophising on the meaning of life, Armenian reed flute playing, Oolong tea drinking, stargazing, Anatolian lace making, wine distillery, playing chess, Ludo or I Spy, trainspotting, planning revolutions, ricotta cheese making, Baguazhang or Indian stick fighting, squirrel and tortoise watching, potion creation from wild herbs, and a whole host of other things the morons on TV think are 'uncool' (yawn), but those of us who actually have a personality and more than a breadcrumb of intelligence can find deeply engaging.

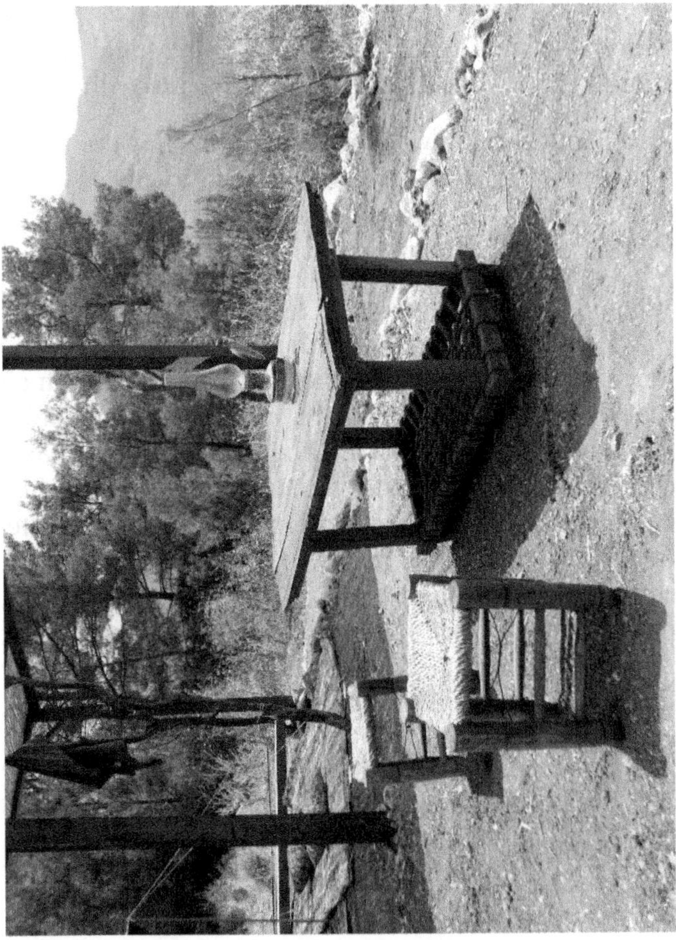

Blogging and Taiwan

September 2013

I might never have dreamed of being an earthbag builder, but I did always harbour a lust for writing. So while some vocations might be unplanned, others are locked in our hearts from the word go. I think I've wanted to write since I was about six years old. Yet, it has always seemed so dauntingly out of reach. There are publishers to convince, cynical editors to win over, networks of the 'right' people to circulate among. I'm not really a circulator. I've never felt particularly congruous with the literati, nor am I able to see the world in the ways that journalistic convention necessitates. I have often felt I must have been born with alien lenses grafted onto my retinas. So I buried my little dream years ago and became a teacher instead. But it was there, it was always there. And then along came the internet.

You'd think that my writing would have immediately found its expression in a blog. Yet, I never saw myself as a blogger. I'd taken it into my head that blogs were the diaries of bored housewives, or the ramblings of conspiracy theorists. My hands, all callouses and scratches, were too dirty for all that typing, my brain not wired for the information technology required. I was completely computer illiterate. Underneath that bank of preconceived ideas subsisted the cornerstone of my prejudice. I thought writing was an art confined to books and newspapers, not something that flashed up on screen. Then, as usual, something in my life went 'wrong', and I was forced to reconsider all of that.

It is just now, as I tip over the first birthday of The Mud, that I remember how and why I started. It all began a long way from my remote mountain roundhouse in Turkey. The Mud actually took off in Taiwan.

It was January 2012. Winter had dug its icy claws into my hillside. The house was up, the roof was on, but my mud plaster wasn't working. I was out of physical energy and out of cash, and a well-paid teaching job in Taiwan was as available as a waiter in Kuşadası. If truth be told, I had no inclination to go East at all. I wanted to finish my house. But with only a thousand dollars left in my account, reality was staring at me hard. And it had a face I didn't like too much, one with haggard jowls and a mouth full of scurvy. So, I buckled up, gritted my teeth, and braced myself for a stint of school teacher confinement in Asia. I have to say, after a year of living under the wide, blue bowl of the Turkish sky, it felt like doing time. Yet, how grateful I am now. Because it was in Taiwan, land of sleek high-speed rails, and hi-tech madness, that my Mud blog was born.

There really can't be two more opposite places on Earth than Turkey and Taiwan. With the exception of Istanbul, which is nearly a country in its own right, Turkey is all boundless space and rural wilderness. It is hirsute men and voluptuous women, exploding emotions and laissez-faire, tea breaks and 'tomorrow'. Things take their time to move upwards in Turkey, just like the olive trees in the fields. Nothing goes to plan. You either learn patience, or you leave. Taiwan, on the other hand, is cluttered and fast. It is an island the size of Belgium with a population dense enough to make a mountain nomad's eyes water. Metropolises back onto each other the length of the west coast. They form long trains of cuboid urbanity, and their streets are tight braids of scooters tied with colourful ribbons of fluorescence. Wherever you go, swarms of people (neither hirsute nor voluptuous) are going there too. Taiwan is convenient. It's also workaholic. At least, I've never worked in any other country where a teacher grafts from 7:50 am until 5 pm.

So, a little over a year ago, I was sitting in front of my classroom monitor in Taiwan repressing the urge to keel over from boredom. The question of why a teacher spends hours in front of a monitor is one you have to go Taiwan to find out. But that's how it was. Instead of just swivelling right and left on my chair and clawing at the window, I decided to do something constructive. I taught myself how to build websites. Now, this was quite an undertaking for someone who two years prior hadn't even known what a PDF file was.

Slowly but surely, The Mud emerged from the swamp of my ignorance. Low and behold, a niche for my dream of writing was sculpted into the ether. Thus, one year on, it's time for a little gratitude towards Taiwan. The money didn't last all that long, and I'm almost certain I'll never teach in a school again. But I thank you Taiwan for technologising the hillbilly so that she can live every aspect of her wildest dreams. I thank all these things that go wrong too. Where would I be without them?

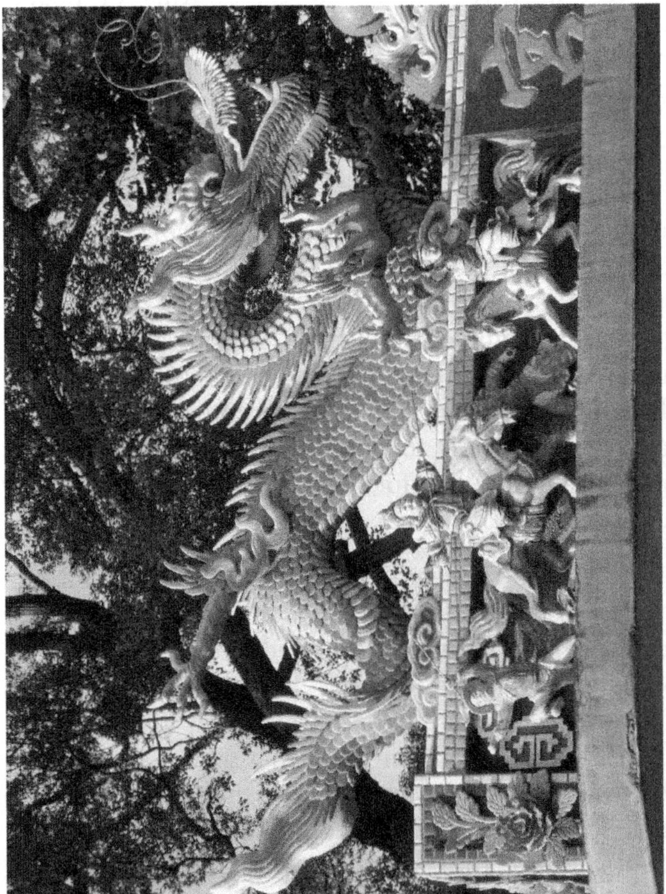

Turning the Clock Back

November 2013

The lid of the night is fixed firmly over the sky. The stars peer through like thousands of shiny, white eyes. The lights of Alakır burn in the distance, faraway lanterns rocking gently in a sea of pitch. Then it begins. The muezzins start the call to prayer, their voices wafting between the mountains like audible morning mist. Too bad if you don't live in a Muslim country. There's nothing quite like their haunting dawn arias.

Back in 2011, when I was living in a tent, that potent pre-dawn awakening was a ritual. It changed the flavour of my entire day. After a while, I moved into my mud house, installed solar panels and light switches, and forgot all about dawn just like everyone else. I would smile when I heard the muezzin call, roll over and go back to sleep.

Yet nothing stays the same in life, does it? Which subconscious demon it was that drew me to the idea, I don't know. One way or another fate conspired, and I did something I had said I never would. I adopted a dog, Rotty. I would kiss goodbye to those lazy, late mornings there and then.

All too soon, it became obvious. The call to prayer was Rotty's cue. Before daylight had so much as stretched a finger over the horizon, she would begin to whimper, then howl, then bark – anything to get me out of bed. How I cursed her! I tried everything to restore the previous order of mornings; I reprimanded her, ignored her, put her close to my bed when I slept outside (she licked me to death in excitement), put her in the kitchen (she cried so mournfully I had to get up). I buried my head under my pillow. I moved inside my earth house to drown out the noise. She scratched my doors and wrecked my walls. Finally, I threw in the towel.

"Agh! Have it your way, Rotty!"

I got up.

I remember that fateful first morning well. The muezzins' chorus coiled around the valley. Rotty's whines spiralled in sync. I groaned. I blinked and stretched. Then I began to fight my way out of my mosquito net. Now, the mosquito net is both an indispensable and simultaneously devilish contraption. It is designed for use by sober, fully-functioning individuals with 20/20 vision. For reasons known only to mosquito net makers, there is no emergency exit. And this is why, if you have to evacuate your net in a hurry, you will fail.

After much flailing about, I gave up trying to find the net's opening and slid commando-style under one edge. Bang! I rolled off the bed, onto the floor. Half of the nylon web came with me. There was some bad language. I disentangled myself, pulled myself up and promptly tripped over Rotty's lead. After all this, I staggered in the direction of the bathroom. The turmoil was all the more unbearable, because Rotty was leaping about squealing in excitement. "This is all *your* fault!" I grumbled, shaking my finger in my pup's face. She sat her bottom in the dirt and wagged her tail inanely.

It was a routine I was to enact every day from then to the present. Even now, each dawn call to prayer, I curse the day I got a dog. Then I fight a blind duel with the mosquito net, fall over a shoe, grumble at Rotty, and stomp off up the hill with her bounding along behind.

But after a few steps, everything changes. From way off east, light begins to pry open the lid of the night. The stars close their eyes one by one. Mountains appear from nowhere with cloaks of fur pulled over their jagged, old shoulders. Birds crank up their morning twitter. I can literally feel the Earth coming alive. Rotty and I will have walked for no more than ten minutes before the sun pushes over the ridge of Moses Mountain. And when it does, the entire valley is washed pink, and then copper, then gold. I turn to Rotty. Now it's my turn to grin inanely. "Oh I'm so glad you got me up for this!" I gush.

I wish I could say that Rotty winks smugly here. She doesn't, because Rotty has no idea why I wouldn't get up at dawn in the first place. Everything that's not nocturnal gets up at dawn. It's only humanity that has gotten out of the habit. And it's true. Ever since I have been rising with the sun again, I have been feeling extraordinarily well, both in body and mind. There's no doubt about it, we are designed for that rhythm. Sales of Prozac would plummet if people simply went to bed and got up a bit earlier.

Which brings me to Winter Time and the invidious reversal of daylight saving. Yes, it's that time of year again. As if we didn't have enough trouble rising with the sun, the government orders us to put the clocks back an hour. Am I the only one to find taking an hour of daylight from a highly productive time of the day, like between 5:30 pm and 6:30 pm, and then wedging it into a predominantly useless time, say between 6:00 am and 7:00 am, fundamentally flawed logic? From the groans I hear each year, it seems I'm not alone. 'Ooh the nights are drawing in now!' We say. There are scowls. 'I hate it when the clocks go back, the days are too short.'

I've often wondered why we do it at all. Back in the UK, there are a couple of minority groups (farmers, and an extinct creature once known as the milkman that only people of a certain age will remember) that dislike daylight saving, because it means darkness until 10 am. And on the basis of those dwindling voices, the entire country puts the clocks back. Other countries like Turkey follow suit so that they stay in sync with European business hours. Yes, we on the Mediterranean are essentially reversing the hands on our timepieces, because a deliverer of milk in 1970s Yorkshire wanted to see the sun rise before he finished his shift. On this basis, one might ask why we don't put the clocks back eight hours instead of just the one, that way night-shift workers in Asda would get a fair deal on sunlight too.

Such is life in a centralised system. Which is why, this year, I decided to put an end to the tyranny and rebelled (nothing new there, some might say). The last Sunday in October came and went, and my clocks remained unchanged.

I wasn't entirely sure how the experiment would unfold. But it soon became apparent that the advantages of holding on to daylight saving are many, and they multiply when you are the only one to do it. Not only do I still enjoy daylight until half past six in the evening, but the banks now open at ten and close at six, which is a lot more convenient if you ask me. No longer do I arrive in town and find the Post Office about to close for lunch. And whenever I meet up with someone, I've always got another hour to spare.

Yet now of course, out from the night of convention, another more profound truth dawns; the arbitrariness of clock time. Yes, be it Winter Time, Summer Time, or Greenwich Mean Time, do I really need a chronometer to schedule when I eat, sleep and work? Hmm. I'll let you know the answer to that next year perhaps, when I throw out my clock instead.

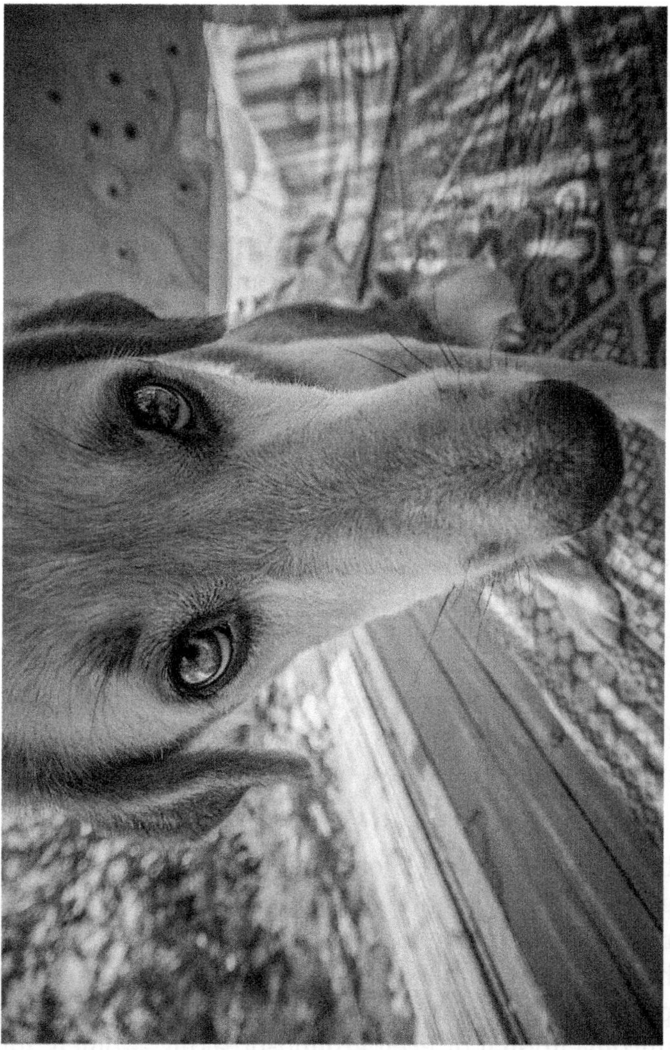

Women Builders

December 2013

I'm ready. My earth walls are thick, in fact they're bullet-proof, which may be just as well, because whenever you approach the subject of gender, you are guaranteed plenty of disagreement. So I'll dive straight in. It might not be what people want to hear, but I say, if you're a woman out there wanting the house of your dreams, the chances are you're not going to get it unless you do it by yourself.

Living the life I do, I've run into many folk who've run from the conventional and galloped into the hills after their dream life. Some are couples. Some are groups. Some are single. Some are continually in transition between all three states. But when it comes to women actually taking a hammer in their hand and constructing their very own dream house, top to bottom, I've only ever seen it happen without a man. (Though I'd love to hear a story where that wasn't the case, so if anyone has got one, let me know.)

Now, I freely admit, I have been the fortunate beneficiary of barrel loads of assistance from both genders in the creation of my home. House-building is rarely a job for the Lone Ranger. Who builds single-handedly? But the question is, who is owning the project? When constructing something unconventional or even ground-breaking, women, for a variety of reasons, tend not to take ownership when there is a man on the scene. And when you don't take ownership, you don't have the final say, which means when it comes to choosing between your dream of a hand-crafted stone wall with natural mud mortar that hasn't been invented yet, or a quicker but less earth-friendly concrete solution, your 'impractical' vision is likely to hit the wayside.

All of this is not necessarily the fault of men. Over the past two years, I have been blessed by streams of benevolent testosterone cascading onto my land; men who have genuinely gunned for me and been there for me when the going has got a little bumpy. But I must add, for the sake of honesty and truth, that there have been deep ravines of misogynist contempt to negotiate, too. Once, before the earthbag adventure, when I was in the Kabak valley and trying to glean how a platform was put together, the builder turned to me and sneered, "You'll never be able to do this." His group of cronies laughed so hard, you'd have thought I was trying to push testicles out of my groin, not understand the hardly brain-stretching logic behind what was basically a wooden gazebo light years from rocket science.

Events like the one above hurt. And it's one (but definitely not the only) reason women stay away from construction. In all honesty, Mr Builder was only voicing a belief that the group subconscious (both male and female) has accepted, no matter how polite a face it puts on it. Please note that I said subconscious. Consciously, many of us want to promote equality of opportunity. The trouble is, women whacking nails in, or revving a chainsaw, is not an image we have been taught to absorb or project (unless it's via a few music videos of buttock-wobblingly dubious content). Women can excel when it comes discrimination, too. How many times have women gone through my site and referred to me as a man!

But let me get the plywood straight, before a thousand and one oestrogen propelled jigsaw blades are whirred in my direction. This isn't about blame. I can be just as bad. What this says to me is, forget the guys, quite a few women don't view women as being able to build. And the reason for this is that there are some deeply-rooted, widely promulgated myths floating through the ether, and they flit in and out of our ears, time and time again. They are in women's heads. They are in men's heads. And they are lethal. I have, at various times in my life, believed some of them. But over the past two years, pretty much every single one has been smashed to genderless smithereens.

Myth 1.

"Women aren't strong enough to build alone."

Oh yeah, the all-time classic. I'm sorry to say even the most well-intentioned are prone to voicing this. Really, shelve this belief right now. We live in the 21st century, and there is a tool for pretty much any job you can think of. And when there isn't? Well, you'd be amazed at just what you can lift or drag when you put your mind to it. In my experience, physical fitness, stamina, lateral thinking and sheer obstinacy are far more useful than size (which rarely equals strength anyway). But whoever you are, however big you are, the more you lift, the stronger you get. If the worst comes to the worst, you can always hire some muscle. This way you retain ownership of the project rather than having to compromise your vision.

Myth 2.

"I have no experience. No one builds without experience."

This is a tough nut to crack. When you have no experience, it's hard to find someone generous enough to let you get your greenhorn mitts on their prized Black and Decker. That's why ultimately, I think women only build alone or in groups of other women. Because it's nigh impossible to get a foot in the door otherwise (though I am indebted to Adam Frost back in 1987 for patiently letting me grapple with his bike spanners and Swarfega, these things are not forgotten).

Myth 3.

"It's much easier just to flirt a bit, and get a guy to do it."

Yeees. It's so very 'convenient' to allow the man in the group to sweat through all the 'difficult' jobs, right? (I raise my hand here, guilty all the way to the compost heap.) Though, seriously, I'm starting to think our human bent for convenience is our worst enemy. It makes slaves of us all. We lose our independence, our muscles and our self-belief for what initially appears to be an easier life, and invariably is the road to ruin. The physically challenging jobs can often be the most rewarding ones, too. You finish the day exhausted but aglow with a feeling of self-confidence and accomplishment. Who needs a gym?

Myth 4.

"When I mess up, I'll be ridiculed until kingdom come because I'm a woman."

This is not a myth. It's absolutely true. One only has to skim through the net to see the unparalleled mockery women are subject to when they make the slightest cock-up in any area considered male. But the beauty is, the derision always seems to come from small, jealous wannabes who've never managed a single gutsy project in their life. So take refuge in that, I know I do. Personally, I've never met anyone that's actually built an eco-home who has criticised anyone else. It's a supportive community. It is also why I proudly display every blunder I have made, because if you haven't made an error, you haven't built a damn thing. You've sat in front of a screen and typed instead.

Myth 5.

"I don't want to build. I can't think of anything worse!"

I have no idea how much of this is self-imposed myth and how much is a genuine dislike of construction. There are presumably people of either gender who have as little desire to build, as I have to organise a dinner party. My poor, long-suffering friend Elif is one of them. No doubt traumatised by my relentless efforts to 'give her a chance' to build (I've had her plastering doors, holding up beams and carrying water tanks), last month she drew the line. When I offered her the drill, she shook her head in outright refusal. "Ooof! I've no idea what you see in all of this!" she said. "Now, I'd like to cook dinner if that's alright with you."

And yes. It was very alright with me. The best I've eaten in a long while.

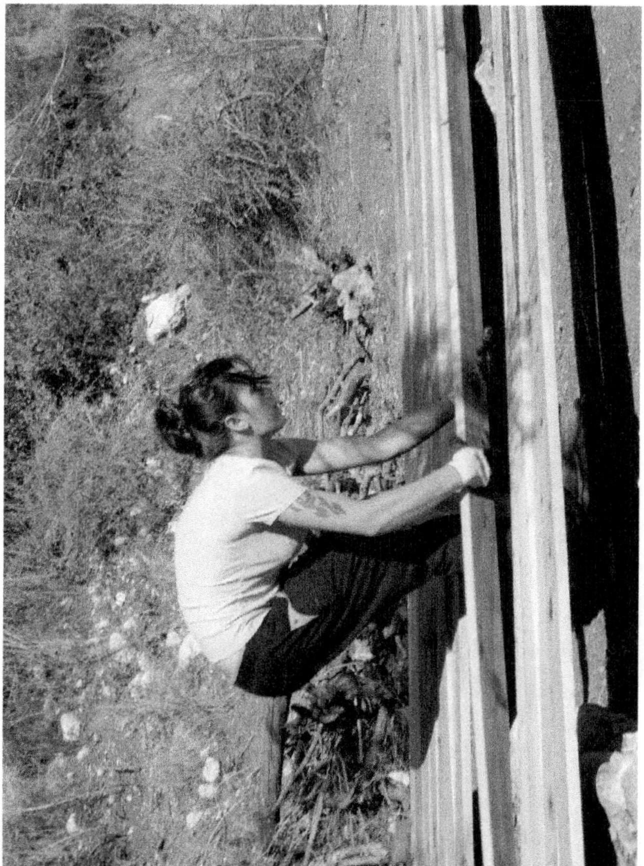

2014

Five Obstructions

January 2014

Long before The Mud, long before earthbag houses and composting toilets, when I was teaching in the Turkish city of Antalya and spending absurd amounts on Penne all'Arrabbiatta and chocolate soufflé, a friend invited me over to watch a Lars von Trier movie. I buckled up and braced myself for two hours of marginally pretentious wallow into the dark side of the human spirit. But I was in for a surprise. Not necessarily about the pretentiousness, but because the film profoundly changed the way I view creativity. OK, all well and good, but what's all this got to do with The Mud Mountain Blog and earthbag houses, and alternative living? Well, because if there's one film you should watch before embarking on a building project, I'd say *The Five Obstructions* is it.

The Five Obstructions is a documentary starring von Trier's mentor, filmmaker Jørgen Leth. To summarize the film very briefly, von Trier sets Leth the task of making five short remakes of Leth's 1967 film *The Perfect Human*. The snag is, each time he issues the suffering filmmaker with an obstruction. One obstruction is that Leth has to remake the film in Cuba and with a maximum shot-length of 12 frames, another is that the film should be a cartoon. It quickly emerges just how crucial the obstruction is to stimulating and guiding Leth's creativity. When, as a punishment for failing to complete an obstruction properly, von Trier tells filmmaker Leth to redo the movie with no obstruction at all. Leth all but throws a fit, blurting something along the lines of 'you can't do that! That's the cruellest thing to do to an artist, give them absolute freedom.'

In the years that followed, I pondered many an hour on Leth's outburst. Because we so often hear the opposite; that artists need to be unfettered in order to create. I, for one, had long entertained the notion that to write, paint or make things, I required a vast open landscape devoid of boundaries and impediments. There were to be no financial limitations, no side job to sequester large portions of my attention, ample time, endless resources, and an ever-supportive, all-positive audience. I thought those were the factors necessary for cultivating the most original ideas. Without obstructions, inspiration could float in like an exotic, vibrant-winged butterfly and then manifest on the page, or the canvas, or in The Mud. But I was wrong. That's not how it works at all. Time has shown me over and over again that it is the obstruction that pushes the creativity gas pedal, not freedom.

So, to return to The Mud. When I first moved onto my beloved 2500 square metres of land back in 2011, it looked just like the undefiled canvas I had coveted. Everything was in abundance: earth, rocks, daylight hours. The sky stretched open and blue like a cloudless door to the God of Great Ideas. The view rolled on and away from me in an unobstructed green tumble. The mountains were so ridiculously steep and bold, they seemed to laugh at the mere suggestion of limitation. I wondered whether it was unethical to lay down rules in such a happy circle of unconstraint. But I loved my spot deeply, and I wanted to protect it. So I made Mud Laws or Mud Obstructions.

The Five Obstructions of The Mud.

1. No concrete is permitted anywhere on the land.

2. No smoking within the borders.

3. No squares and straight lines.

4. No killing of animals.

5. No major expense.

I'm not going to spend time defending the whys and wherefores of each obstruction. None of them exist as moral condemnations. They are my preferences. And the beauty of owning your own land is that you're entitled to a little caprice. What is more exciting is the creativity each obstruction has fostered. Not being able to use concrete, for example, generated a wealth of bright ideas regarding mortar, mosaic grouting and house foundations. The banning of corners, though not always successfully obeyed (I'm eons from the architect Hundertwasser) resulted in a house that makes me sing when I sit in it, and simultaneously strong enough to withstand earthquakes. My budget was instrumental in producing some of the most inspired parts of the home, as either the natural resources on my land or other people's rubbish became my materials. Broken tiles, grass, bottles, branches, reeds, thrown-away cupboards, broken windows, cracked crockery and reject furniture all turned into an enchanting game of 'now what can we make out of that'. Banning smoking (and in a country like Turkey an outdoor smoking ban is none too easy to implement) changed the entire dynamic of the land. It affected something beyond the physical, and my space became a place of creation or peaceful contemplation, rather than busy socialisation.

I write all this because normally, when problems and limitations arise, we are so apt to feel stymied. In fact, one of the attractions of writing over building is that ideas can remain just that; perfect bubbles of non-matter, before they are subject to the humiliating degradations of the physical world. But Gaia (and von Trier come to mention it) have changed my perspective on the art of creation. In construction, time, money, available materials, energy and the weather are the big five obstructions everyone has to face. Sometimes rain calls off play. Other times it's just too hot to lift a rock. Sometimes you simply can't find the power to bang in another nail. It gets dark and you haven't managed to finish the plastering. The roof beams cost three times more than you'd hoped. These are all construction classics and so often result in frustration. These days, I look at such obstructions as my friends rather than my enemies. Who knows? Perhaps they were stuck onto the canvas of the Earth just to prod our otherwise lethargic imaginations. And perhaps von Trier has a right to a little pretention, as well.

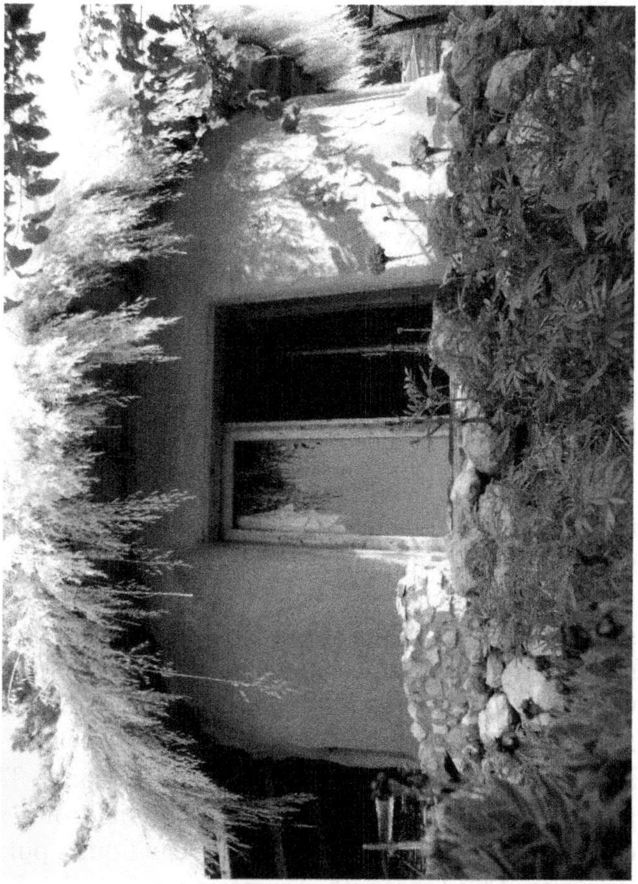

Fear and the Other World

February 2014

Not everyone who relocates into the wilds is content. There are many who buy land, build houses and wind up just as dissatisfied as they were before, sometimes more so. I've heard one or two say they felt so traumatised by the experience they moved back to the city.

Nature is an awe-inspiring, plan-crunching, target-ignoring, and largely unsentimental beast. It can also be the most accepting, supportive and rejuvenating friend. As far as I can see, the deciding factor is the human spirit.

After 'Don't you get lonely?' the next most frequently voiced question to me is 'Don't you get scared?' Yes, sometimes quite frankly, I do. On a moonless winter night, a night so dark that even the shadows are in hiding, my road turns from a scenic strip of nobbled red earth into the gulf of Hades. Occasionally, I'll walk up that road to a friend's house. Sporadic blips of orange poke through the rucks of the hillside opposite; lights from the hamlet nearby. They give the valley the appearance of something from *Lord of the Rings*, and for some reason I can't quite put my finger on, I find that rather comforting. But it's when I reach the top that the background music changes.

There, at the triangular junction where my dirt track and a tarmac road meet, is the cemetery. By day it's the quaintest village cemetery you are ever likely to see; a random clutter of small graves nestled in a mountainside olive grove. The dead occupy a glorious vista with the Mediterranean in the distance. But by night? There's no sea view, no olive trees, only the vague outline of gravestones poking up from the inky soil. I always stride past that graveyard doing my utmost not to search out shadows moving beyond the stone wall. Then, I hear the dog, or rather the local hound from hell. It belongs to the shepherd who lives in the web of wooden struts and plastic up the bank.

The dog has smelt my fear and is now burning a trail of snarling carnage in my direction. I start running. I reach the turn-off to my friend's house, the barking growing closer by the minute. I flick my torch back and see the dog's eyes; two soulless glass buttons flashing in a cloak of endless black. I can't see the teeth. But it doesn't matter. I know what they're like; huge flesh-ripping, saliva-coated fangs rasping to get stuck into my leg. The torch becomes a weapon. I flick the beam towards the eyes and dazzle the dog for a few seconds. I use those moments to back as quickly as I can down the track.

Scared? I'm so mortally petrified it will take a good half hour before I utter a sentence without a swear word.

Yet, nothing at all has really happened. The dog hasn't killed me. It didn't even reach me. There were no zombies in the graveyard, and no cold hands stretching out from the graves. If I draw the dark half of my mind to one side and peer beyond it, I see the night is an open face spattered with freckles of starlight. The darkness is a mystery that the pine trees are now pumping life into. And the sky is wise and profound. I am part of that dark, profound mystery. I am breathing it.

Alone in the wilds these things will happen. Boar may come cantering out of the forest and nose round your tent for a midnight snack. You may be faced with winds rushing at 60 kilometres an hour, and all you have over your head is a sliver of flapping canvas, or perhaps the track into your land has morphed into a mud slick and you realise you might not be able to leave for three days. In such situations, bravado and a few positive affirmations just aren't going to cut the mustard. Nor is a gun, a torch, or a dog. You need other sturdier tools in your psychological toolbox if you want to mitigate the panic.

Personally speaking, to truly derive the immense pleasure available from the natural world, and to be able to reconnect with it without dissolving into a blubbering wreck, I have needed a practice. For me, that practice is meditation in general, Vipassana more specifically. Though sometimes a few yoga asanas will do the trick as well. Now, I'm not a meditation or yoga evangelist (been there, done that). The meditation malarkey is simply one of many ways to deal with the fog of fear and worry that can quickly blanket the human spirit when things don't appear to be as they should. Other people have other techniques; walking barefoot on the earth, t'ai chi, hiking.

Once the fog clears, I can reconnect, not just with the Earth, but with the thing that underpins it all. I'd call that thing the spiritual world for want of a better phrase. The trouble with words is they drag so many connotations behind them. A word is never just a word. It's a story. What I'm trying to allude to when I use the words 'spiritual world', is not a belief system, nor a religion, nor angels and devils, nor pixies and wood sprites. For me, the word 'spiritual' refers to everything that is not physical. Things you can't see, hear, feel, touch or smell. I could use the term 'non physical' world, but that implies a 'non' event, or an absence of something. The Other World that lies beyond the senses is not a nothing, it's a whopping great something, and without it, whether you live in a tent in the hills or in a basement flat in a honking city, there's not much difference. Sorry, scratch that. There's light-years of difference! Nonetheless, it's the spiritual element that defines the quality of the experience.

The most obvious element of the spiritual world is thought; ideas, concepts and images in the human mind. Thoughts hold no physical space. They can't be touched, smelt or seen by others. Yet they are the most powerful element of the human being and shape the very fabric of our lives. For most of us, thought is based on two drives; fear and desire. Freud called it the pleasure principle, the endless psychological struggle to seek out pleasure and avoid pain. Vipassana meditation talks about craving and aversion. Watch your thoughts for any given moment and it's easy to see; either the mind is galloping down a track of worry and strategising how to avoid trouble, or it's chasing after a dream and fantasising. And if there isn't a memory of a real experience for the mind to grasp onto, it will use those plied to it by the media and advertisers instead.

So when you arrive in your wilderness paradise, nature will be there waiting for you with her well of magic and nourishing secrets. But will you see her? When a gale force wind begins to crush your dome tent, will you feel awe, or simply terror? Will you trust your instincts, and the movement of the land around you? Or will you be overtaken by the images generated by any number of horror films? For me, it is often a very fine line. The only way I can cross that line is to sit each morning, breathe, watch my mind spouting its gibberish, see through it and sense the vast benevolent power of the spiritual realm within. Without that, I know I wouldn't be here. I would have packed my bags two-and-a-half years ago and run away as fast as I could.

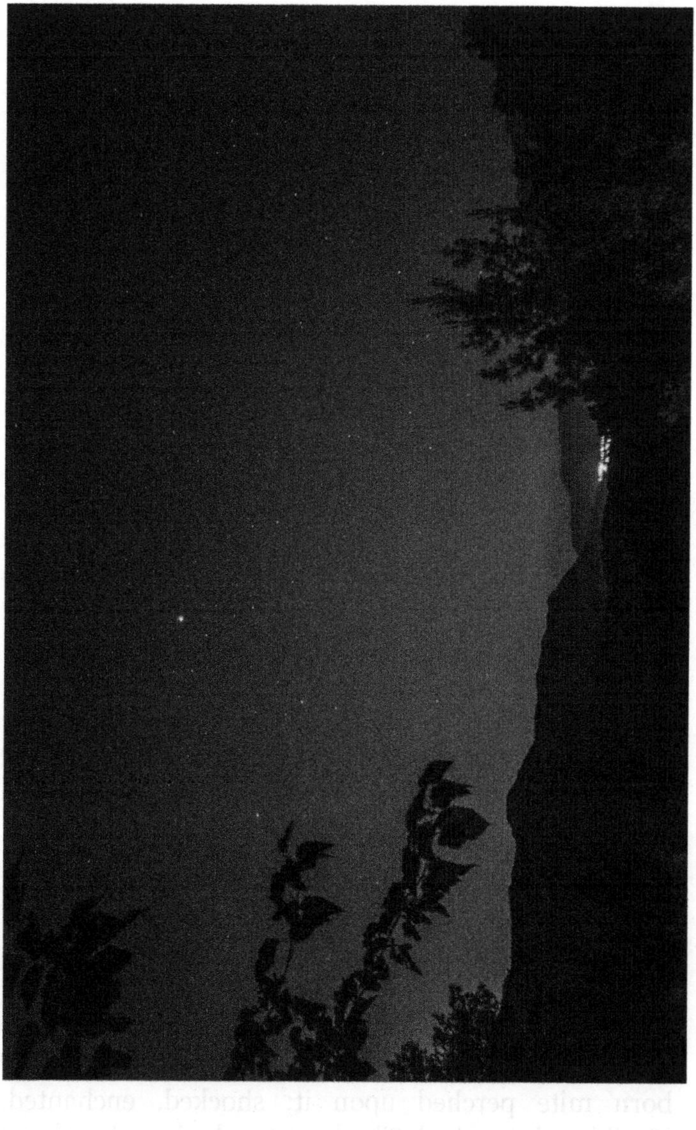

The Perils of the Comfort Zone

April 2014

'Life begins at the end of the comfort zone'.

This was what was scribbled on a note taped to our fridge door back in Taiwan 2010. And yes, I liked the adage, because I saw it as a call to climb out of the rut, drop the known in the nearest dustbin, and trot baggage-free after a risk. I remembered the sentence a couple of months ago, because for the past three years I think I've been living it in reverse. I'm starting to wonder if comfort and deep fulfilment are mutually exclusive.

If the comfort zone is a circle, or even an ellipse like the orbit of the Earth round the sun, then life up here in The Mud started far outside it. The moment I brought my tent up here and cleared my 2 x 3 metres of space into the brambles, I had hacked a hole into another world. That world was just about inside the solar system of my experience. I was still in Turkey after all. But it was definitely on the outer edge, somewhere just past Pluto.

When I first slept outside and grappled with washing-up racks and wheelbarrows of water, comfort, both spiritual and physical, was a distant speck on a horizon I was walking in the other direction of. Everything was for the first time. It was pristine yet wild. My world was a dew drop at 5 am, and I was a new born mite perched upon it; shocked, enchanted, bewildered, touched. The land touched me because I had no walls erected against it. No expectations. No great vision of what it 'should' be. Those first months were magical. Trees muttered in crackles and rustles. Mysterious plants snuck out of the dust to feed me, or heal me. Butterflies, lizards and bugs crawled from the rocks with secret messages. The night sky was alive with other worlds. I was Alice in Wonderland.

What is it with us humans and our preoccupation for 'the rut'? I know very well, routines are the orderly assassins of magic, yet now, with the house of my dreams, running water and solar power, I start to find myself unconsciously retreating from 'the new' and sliding back into the dull predictability of the organised. Now that I'm all comfy in my Earth womb, like a marine in a dugout, or a one of those reptiles in their holes, Eden gradually withdraws. It's down to my outside kitchen and bathroom keep me on my toes. While it's uncomfortable to cook in a raging storm, it's also incredibly visceral. I love that I have to face storms for a cup of tea, or grab my brolly to take a leak. Apparently we need to face the elements just to remember we're connected to them and enlivened by them. Even so. I feel those old days of wonder sliding from under my fingertips, and I miss them. Yes, the comfort zone is coming for me, loping and slobbering with couch-potato dissatisfaction.

Which was why I sent a wish out into the valley not so long back. 'Don't let me become complacent, Gaia, whatever you do,' I said. Be careful what you wish for, they say. Because life, the ol' trickster, is always waiting...right over the edge of your comfort zone.

Two weeks ago, something happened that blew complacency all the way to kingdom come. My novel *Ayşe's Trail* took off, and I have to leave here temporarily for London. Despite this being a childhood dream come true, for the first few days after receiving the news, I was beset by deep melancholy. As I wandered about my queendom of olives and home-grown veg and lizards, I began to fret about where all this book lark was leading me. I don't want to leave the forest, and I feel an irrational and fearful urge to cling on. This place has brought me such happiness. It has healed me. The thought of hitting the big city, having to dress up and possibly participate, even temporarily, in a lifestyle I've long left behind, leaves me panic-stricken and morose.

But when fear decides a course of action, nothing good follows. Just as my garden and the forest about me changes with every year, so do I. Am I really going to hide in a cave forever and refuse to grow or put my hand out into the light? Because nothing around me accepts such self-imposed stifling. So last week I took a deep breath. I kissed the earth and hugged my home. Then I let my expectations of it go, because that's the only proper thing to do when you're in love with something. Free it. As I did, I heard the comfort zone growl, before it withdrew reluctantly back into its lair. At that moment, the wind of life was in my hair again, and adventure howled down from the hills. The moon was eclipsed, the stars swung into new patterns, and the pines curled and twisted on their roots. I have no idea where I'm going, or what will happen next. But I expect it'll be worth writing about.

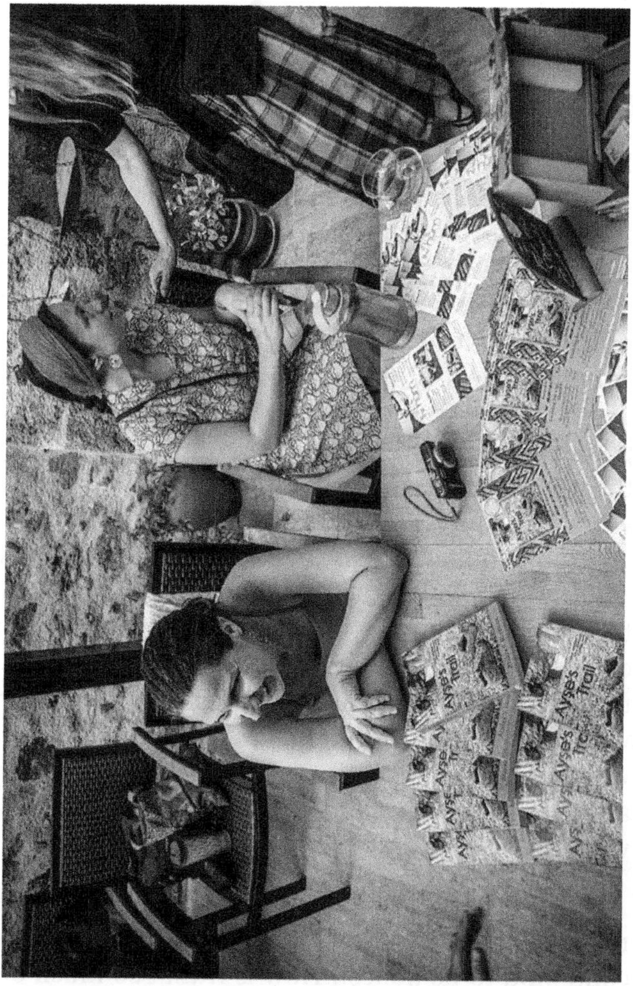

Where Did Environmentalism Go Wrong?

May 2014

There's an atmosphere of despair pervading the environmental movement at the moment. And if it's stats you go by, then it's no wonder. According to *National Geographic*, more than 80% of Earth's natural forests have already been destroyed, *eighty per cent*, most of it very recently. 38% of the world's surface is under threat of desertification, and in a recent in-depth NASA study measuring drastic changes to population, climate, water, agriculture, and energy in the 21st century, some sort of collapse in about fifteen years is likely. Well, yes, it really doesn't take an environmental scientist to see that if the population continues to explode at its current rate and we have no trees left, we won't be breathing. No doubt a corporation will produce oxygen and sell it on to the masses at an exorbitant rate. Those who can afford it will have it pumped into their homes, those who can't will slowly die off. What's new? That's the way it already is with drinking water in large parts of the world.

Feeling desperate? Join the club. I've been feeling more than a little despair myself, despair mixed with contempt, to be honest. How is it that so much of the world still refuses to even face the issue at hand, I've been wondering, never mind act on it? How can people possibly still be bleating about cellulite or the private life of celebrities when their entire existence is in the balance? Is this a type of mass lunacy?

Yet, if I can set my anger aside, the truth is not a question of intelligence. It's obvious. Humanity is in denial. And that is, in fact, quite normal. Despite living in a mud hut, I'm probably just as much involved in it. Anyone who has lost someone close knows, the first reaction to a terminal prognosis is to pretend it just isn't happening, because the truth is simply too devastating to contemplate. Everyone focuses on the hope that there will be a miracle, or some sudden technological innovation, or perhaps the doctors were wrong. Unfortunately, as I myself have witnessed, denial doesn't prevent truth from dawning. Terminal patients still die, as we all do, be it today, tomorrow, or in fifteen years.

It is here that I'd like to pause. Because, although this is all true, it is also, as I see it, one of the gravest strategic errors the environmental movement has made since the beginning. With an unwavering fascination with the end of the world, environmentalism has attempted to scare humanity into acting, and we are now seeing just how spectacularly scare tactics have failed. Not that the scare isn't based on solid foundations, it's more that apparently, scared people are not particularly effective at mobilising. Humanity has been plunged into despair, and so it has buried its head even deeper in the sand of any one of our expanding deserts.

I've often thought that environmentalism, for all its railing against consumerism and the materialism that fuels it, is in fact over-obsessed with the material and under-obsessed with the soul, and that the fate of our planet simply cannot be altered without a deeper understanding of why we are sabotaging it. Environmentalism should have taken a leaf out of the book of its far more successful sibling in the 'ism' family, capitalism. How did capitalism beat environmentalism? It perused a bit of Freud and worked out what made us tick. It offered a carrot, where the environmentalists, who've been all hellfire and brimstone, have offered none. Either we fight off the forces of massive earth-devouring corporations with nothing more than a yaks' wool jumper and a couple of placards, or we face certain death. Well thanks for that inspiring choice. Don't mind me if I ship in a case of Chateauneuf-du-Pape and drink myself into oblivion.

I have blabbered before on the two drives that the human mind finds itself caught between; desire and fear (prodded by the carrot or stick mentioned above). The mind, despite its façade of sophistication, is a primitive, largely reptilian beast. When desire seems easier to attain than fear is to dispel, then the mind weighs up the odds. 'What I fear is coming regardless, I may as well grab some of what I want', it bargains. Environmentalism and its use of the media has unwittingly created a bottomless pit of angst within the human spirit, and I'm sorry, but you can't save the world on that. To really be able to achieve a miracle (and seeing as I've witnessed a few, I view them as entirely possible, though not inevitable) the mind needs to be in a very different place. It needs to feel confident. It needs to be saturated in realistic rather than foundationless hope. And it helps one hell of a lot, if somewhere along the line a nice fat desire is fulfilled. If people will slave away for weeks in miserable jobs merely to possess an iPhone, the satisfaction of which lasts less than a month, what might they do for a greater prize? But if there is no prize? Then what are they striving for?

Environmentalism has offered a prize of sorts, but it's been fairly puritanical about it. The prize is an abstract salvation, which to the average human feels as remote as the Delta Quadrant and as likely as Eldorado. Environmentalism is just like any religion in its complete inability to curb the desires of humanity with a heaven and hell scenario, merely producing a state of guilt among its followers instead.

Now, this isn't supposed to be a diatribe on the ills of environmentalism, because without the environmental movement our awareness of the issue at hand would be zilch. It is the brave and devoted ecologists in the Green movement who have collected the data. It's just that if anything at all is to be done, we have to recognise the old way of blame and protest isn't working.

If The Mud Mountain Blog and has a purpose or a hope or a vision at all, it's this. I'd like to paint an alternative, and to show the real carrot that capitalism has usurped, the carrot that environmentalism ought to be grabbing back and waving in front of us for all it's worth. For me, abandoning consumerism and loving the Earth has nothing to do with virtue. There is no moral high-ground to be attained, and no point in burdening oneself with guilt for buying a plastic bag or leaving a light on. Every human being, just like every living thing on the planet uses resources, and if humanity can sense the connection it has with the Earth, then the using of resources can be a beautiful exchange.

I didn't build a mud hut and grow my own beans to save the world. I did it to save myself. Certainly, living simply and in harmony with nature benefits everyone, but no one more than me. And my prize hasn't been some vague whiff of planetary survival eons from today, it is immediate gratification, something I wasn't actually expecting. If you allow it, the wilderness will grant you the deepest sense of happiness you are ever likely to experience. It's even better than sex, actually. Ah, now I've got your attention, haven't I? The modern obsession with sex is a direct indication of the impoverishment and boredom of day to day living, and the deep lack of connection most people experience.

Yes. I will say it again. And again. And again. I have lived here with no partner, no car, no road, at times no power and no water, and they were the most exquisite days of my life. Nothing has bettered it. Not drink, not drugs, definitely not the hallowed 'relationship'. Job titles, possessions and bank balances are just trash by comparison. The magic that pours out of the dirt can heal anything. The smell of the grass, the winking of any variety of flowers, the chatter of the leaves, the secrets the animals tell, the protection your special space bestows upon you and the peace of mind it brings you, are incomparable. You will witness miracles and sorcery and beauty. You will feel valuable and safe. Anxiety recedes. Confidence grows. Without the petty distractions of the media and retail, your soul blooms into something magnificent and indestructible. You begin to manifest exactly what you want and need, because your mind becomes a vessel of clarity rather than a cloudy swamp of befuddlement. You are alive and you are life. Every single thing that a corporation is trying to sell you is nothing but a fake version of what is out here in the forest, and it's free. Absolutely free. You need never do a job you hate again.

So if I were you, I'd waste no time. Because if you haven't felt this, you haven't lived. Forget the Top Ten Places You Have to Visit and the Top Ten Films You Have to Watch, there's one thing you should do before you die, and that's sense the wonder of our planet. Sense who you really are. Sense where you came from and what you are truly capable of. Find the wild man or woman within. Go and camp for a night under the stars. Grow endangered plants on your balcony. Ride your bike through the forest and inhale a little unpolluted air. Because you might die tomorrow. Or maybe in fifteen years. And until enough people experience this, there can be no environmentalism, and no one can save anything, because the truth is, most of us have no idea what we're saving.

Mess and the Tree Guru

June 2014

Things were very different when I moved up onto my land nearly three years ago; I was a teacher, a yogi, and disillusioned with both. So I was in a mess. I had joined the teaching profession two decades previous, and like many teachers, it was with the intention of benefitting the human race in some way. After twenty years, I was questioning whether I did ever actually benefit anyone, or merely participate in a system fundamentally damaging to the human spirit. Then there was the other disillusionment with what I shall term 'yogi-ism' (as opposed to the art of yoga). The realisation had dawned on me that no matter how inspiring the teaching, it inevitably becomes a religion. There is a poorly cloaked aura of superiority that surrounds the spiritual climber. 'Do as I preach, not as I do' is an unspoken premise of pretty much every guru around. Except for one.

Nature.

Nature is what it is. It doesn't have a self-image to protect, nor a living to earn. It doesn't need followers, nor praise, nor a curriculum. It doesn't care a hoot about concepts like good or bad. It just is.

I remember one of my first 'awakenings' up here in this small square of Eden. It was the time I suddenly began to see everything the other way up. It was as though I'd been wearing my life inside out for the past forty years. It happened under my 'grandmother' olive tree. It's a wonderful tree with a peculiarly stout, straight trunk. Olives normally possess gnarled old branches that coil like dry bark snakes. But for reasons best known to nature, my grandmother olive tree has a pine's trunk. She's proud and upright holding bundles of leaves in her rich branch hands. Naturally, with all that foliage she is the best sunshade on the land. One of the first things I had done once my camp was established was to sling a hammock between her and another olive tree up the bank.

That day I was swinging in the hammock watching the pomegranates ripening in the field next door, and feeling glum. Nothing had worked out how I wanted it to. My plans had gone up in flames. I didn't want to teach any more but had no idea what else to do to keep the coppers rolling in. I was living in a tent. The mayor had just refused me water. My life felt like a mess. As I rocked, I looked at the other olive tree the hammock was tied to. Unlike the grandmother tree, this one has nowhere near the strength or classic aesthetic appeal of her sister. She's a twisted old crone by comparison. Her branches are weak and full of knots, her trunk has split into three and she's hanging onto a poor display of leaves. I closed my eyes feeling more than a little empathy.

But when, a few seconds later, I opened my eyes again, I began to see it differently. From my rope bed, I scanned the vista of trees on the upper part of the land, and behind there into the forest. Bent pines sent branches jutting off asymmetrically this way and that. Olive trees were stunted. Prickly Mediterranean oak bushes exploded in the gaps like a mess of hag's hair. Nothing followed any sense of decorum, nor any human preconceptions of orderliness. The word 'mess' turned over and over in my head. I realised my life and nature had quite a lot in common.

I blinked again. Then that wise old gal Gaia started talking. You see, nature is beautiful. Intoxicatingly, uncontrollably, irrationally, unreasonably beautiful. The greens, the browns, the ochres, the burnt siennas, the patterns, the non-patterns, the clutter, the spaces, the hollows, the glades, the carpets of pine needles, the dust, the speckles of flowers, the dried up stalks. It's magical and enlivening and transformative.

I've learned so many things from nature, it will take me a lifetime to whisper her secrets. But one of them was that about mess. Mess isn't a bad thing at all. In fact, mess is where the truth happens, the stuff that tests your mettle, the stuff that makes you shriek in wonder and jump up and down in delight. So if your life is a mess, I say wallow in it. Yes, drink in the unruly chaos of it all. Tidiness is for robots not humans.

For me, it's taking a while for that little nugget of nature wisdom to sink in. In truth, I have issues with mess. I like things to look just right. Everything has its place. But I am slowly starting to get it. That everything already looks just right, and is already in its place. Because nature just is. It's not a climber. It's not a wannabe. It's an evolver. And these days I see. They are not the same thing at all.

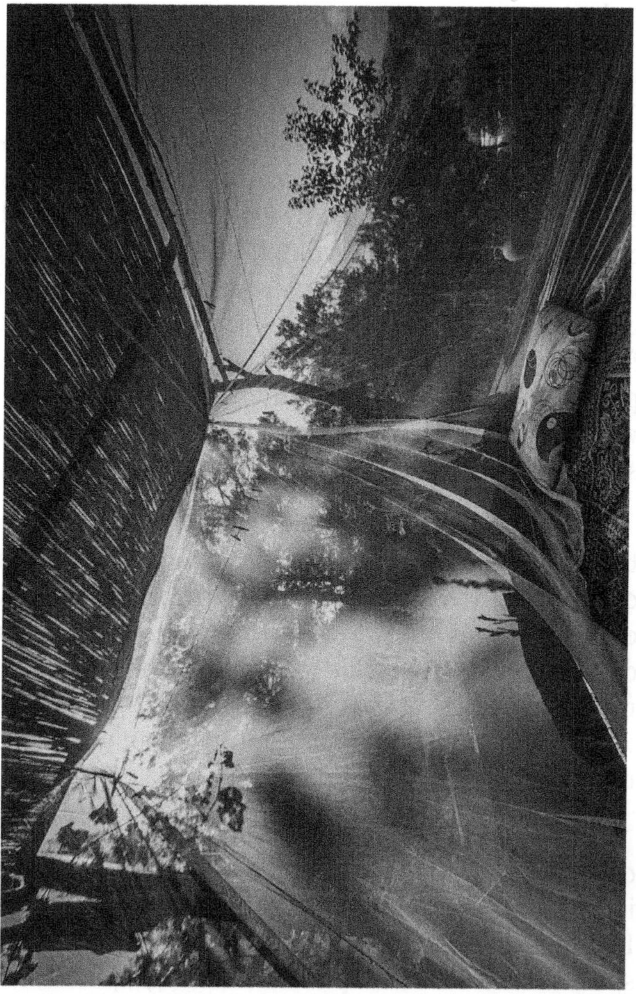

The Well of Me

In honour of genuine selfishness

July 2014

I walked onto this land alone, just as we walk onto this planet alone. We are alone. Always. From birth to death. That solitude terrifies people so deeply, they will put up with the most tedious company to avoid it. Even the word 'alone' rattles coldly when said. Aloneness has come to equal isolation, vulnerability and even danger in the human mind. This may or may not be something inherent in the human condition; we are pack animals, like dogs and lions and...and wolves. Yes wolves are pack animals too. Even so there are lone wolves. So what about them? The ones that roam wild in the steppes compromising to no one?

Alone, just like so many words, has become clichéd to such an extent, most of us have long lost the essence of its truth. It's all hearsay and horror stories. If you close your eyes and say the word 'alone', which image do you see? A small child excluded at the corner of the room? Cold nights with no one to hold? No one there when you need help? No one caring about you? No one understanding you?

When I walked onto this land alone, one woman, one tent, one wheelbarrow, I felt the cold hand of isolation. I was becoming quite the misanthropist. Human beings were self-serving hypocrites; a waste of space on this beautiful planet. A scourge, parasitic and useless. I couldn't understand how no one seemed able to face up to the fact that they were, despite their partners and children and parents and friends, alone. Completely alone. No one is ever going to be 100% on our side, because first and foremost they're on their own side. No one understands another, either. It's impossible. No one can climb into someone else's head and body and experience them. We are the one and only who can do that. We are unique. That uniqueness makes us both incredibly valuable, and alone.

I used to find this abhorrent. What a miserable species we are, I mused. So I took up a pick and a shovel, and hacked myself a space on the Earth. My tent pushed up from the dust like a blue blister in a desert of meaninglessness. Days went by. The digging ate my bitterness. The earth sucked in my anger. I started slowly to shelve the notions I'd learned from books or schools or spiritual philosophies, and opened my eyes to what actually is.

Issues of aloneness are really issues of self. Because there's a core of us that's so very precious, and it cries out to be taken care of. I was angry because humans were selfish, but I soon noticed in nature everything is selfish too. Forget this nonsense of saintly trees giving their fruit freely and expecting nothing in return. Presumably, on a mental level a tree doesn't 'expect' in the way a human does, but it is obvious to anyone who works and lives with plants that if you don't water them or nourish them, a tree will bear you no fruit. A tree takes care of itself first. It makes sure its roots are nice and deep. In fact, no plant will bear you anything unless it has enough for itself. The fruit is a surplus. Animals are the same. With the exception of mothers and their infants, animals feed themselves first, unless they are part of a pack with a hierarchy, in which case they allow the Alpha first pick in return for his or her protection.

The problem is not selfishness. Selfishness is natural. The problem is our attitude to it, and the way we attempt to conceal it, because we've been told it's wrong. Some stuff it in a cupboard and bolt the hatch nice and tight. They help everyone and everything else in the hope that they will be liked, or loved, or approved of, or good and not evil. They become thwarted and undernourished. Suddenly, they are starving. And that starvation moves in two ways; excessive greed or oozing resentment. I have been both greedy and resentful at various times in my life.

Then there are the others, the sociopaths, who have found the moral high ground of the anti-selfish brigade so hopelessly lofty, they turn the other way, shut off their empathy and go for the capitalist kill. These folk will also tell you selfishness is natural. Yet, they confuse natural self-preservation with exploitation, and there's nothing natural about that, as a cursory camp in the wilds will soon tell.

Nature is steeped so deep in wisdom, I wonder why I didn't see it years before. Why did I just listen to the prescribed laws of human culture? Why not just open my eyes? It always seems to take a disaster. Something in our oh-so-fallible human plan has to go dramatically wrong. Then we pause, and ask, 'Is this really the way?' My nice little idea of philanthropy had gone wrong. It just didn't seem to work. So I pulled out of the world and onto my land to think about that for a while.

I have written a lot about nature's magic, but it has a dark side too. I watched aphids rip off baby orange leaves, agama lizards fight for territory, owls pick off rodents, and trees I'd planted and watered give nothing in return. One day, Apo the Anatolian shepherd stole the food out of my little Rotty's bowl. I wondered briefly if mob rule was our lot. If it's destiny for the powerful to pulverise the weak. But that's not how it works in nature. No. Because nature hasn't vilified selfishness.

Nature is selfish, but up to a point, and that point is the point of surplus. Once there's enough, be it territory or food, then nature shares around. Agama lizards don't attempt to expand their territories endlessly. Trees don't hang onto apricots once they've ripened. Owls don't gorge on rats to the extent they become so obese they can't fly. That's the kind of folly humans become embroiled in. Even Apo has been known to take bread to his girlfriend. It is because we've forgotten the art of being naturally selfish that we have also lost the sense of when enough is enough.

The first time I decided to embrace total selfishness, and do whatever I wanted, I remember an initial shiver of terror. I think it was the anticipation of being shunned by others. Being selfish brings it home. If we are looking after number one, it implies everyone's looking after number one, which implies, shock horror, that we are all alone. And we are. Whether we tie each other up in marriages, or move into friendships with an underlying expectation of something coming back, it makes no difference. We are alone. Sooner or later we're reminded. Perhaps there's a limit of money or time. Perhaps two friends are both going through a difficult patch simultaneously, and neither can be there for the other. Perhaps we just can't understand the person we're living with, or they can't understand us.

Yet selfishness didn't work out how I expected, at all. Because three years on, never have I experienced such community! I was inflexible in setting my boundaries. I gave firm instructions that I was not to be disturbed in the morning, and sent people off if they broke the rule. I designated 'me' days, and spent plenty of time by myself. The more I did, the more I loved it. Now I enjoy a strong, varied and stimulating network of friends who all know what I'm like, and accept me for it.

So instead of running full pelt away from solitude, and viewing loners like myself as freaks or anti-social or jaded, why not get to the crux of the issue? Have another look at that phantom of aloneness. Because nowadays, for me, when I hear the word 'alone' I see a silent star-filled night above me with no one interrupting it. I see a home of mud filled with love. I see space to grow on and on without end. I see zero compromise and boundless freedom. I see utter spontaneity with no need to justify or explain. I see the real me. Not the one who performs, not the one that fits in to any given social environment, the me that loves peace and mystery and beauty. The well of me I want to sink deeper and deeper into. The sky of me that I want to fly in. And the more I get to know me, the more I love me. Because when I move beyond the voices in my head, the internalised opinions of other people, I find something else deeply wonderful. A light. A warmth. A joy. Call me selfish, but I'm my own best friend.

Then I wake up one day and find I'm full. I'm satisfied. Nourished. There's a surplus of energy, or ideas or time; a desire to share. So I write a blog, or a book. Perhaps you will pick it off the web, perhaps you won't. It doesn't matter. I didn't sell my soul to create it. This wasn't an agreement we made prior. It's just there, hanging like the first apricot on my tree. If you like the taste, you are welcome to it.

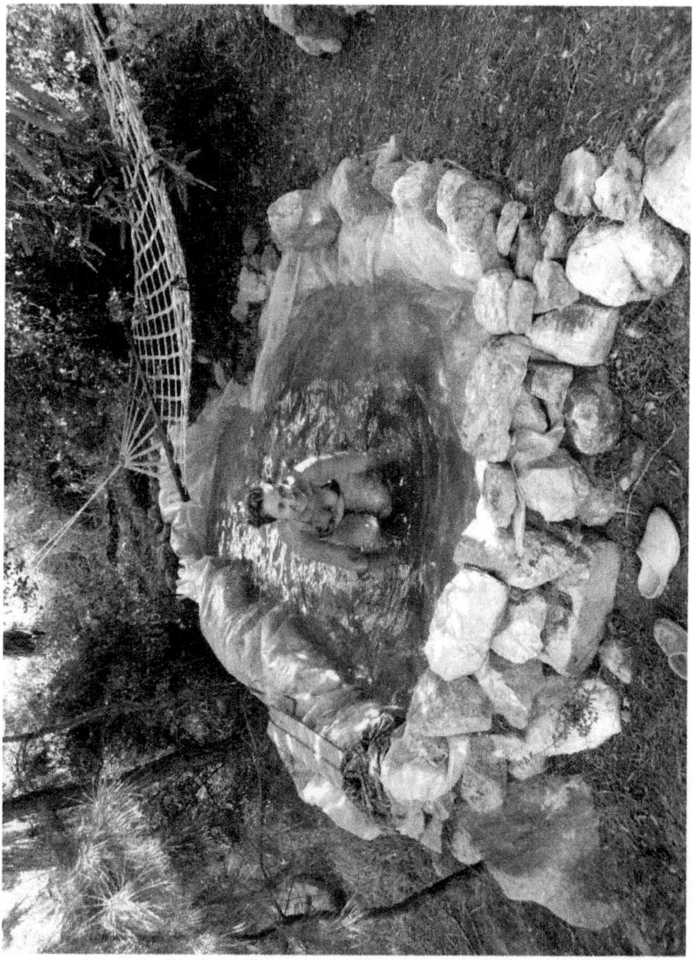

Co-creating Paradise

August 2014

The view rolls away from my house like a pine green double-knot, hand-woven runner. It slides over the mountain sides, into valleys, over hillocks. Its green edge frays at the sea. All around, crickets chirp deliriously, and the forest throbs with their mantra. Beyond that is the tap tap tap of a woodpecker as it digs into the great pine over-head. A light breeze pushes up the land. It plays with the marigolds and the basil turning their leaves like windmills. I inhale. It is pine sap that I smell.

I pull on a rope. The hammock swings to and fro over my small natural pool. I close my eyes. The thoughts uncoil in the space.

Heaven. This is heaven. I have everything I could ever want. All many people want. This is heaven on Earth, and I created it. With my mind. With my hands. With my heart and soul. With my land. And with a little help from something else I really don't understand, something I will perhaps erroneously term the light of inspired action.

Humankind is so powerful. We have the power within us to create almost anything: heaven, hell, mediocrity, beauty, castles, mud palaces, concrete boxes, slums. We are wellsprings of such infinite potential, oceans of wonder and mystery. How is it that we have allowed ourselves to be taken in by the superficial and the addictive, the gross and the empty, the negative and the ugly? If we are really this powerful, how is it so many humans are not creating what they want? Are they flawed? Are they unlucky? Are they simply the bottom of the positive thinking class?

Positive thinking evangelists will have us believe that to create anything we want, all we have to do is imagine it, affirm it, believe it. To a certain extent it's true. But in my personal experience, it's not enough. I rate my personal experience highly, because it's the only window to reality I have. Yes, I've seen that our perception of the world transforms it, and I can attest that a positive, can-do attitude goes a long way to creating amazing things. But it's only half of the story. What's the other half?

There is a skew in worldview particularly prevalent in the West that we are in control. This control 'freakism' has pervaded all manner of new age dogmas, despite their protests against it. In the philosophy of positive thinking, we have ideas and then 'imprint' them on reality – as if reality were a lifeless object with nothing better to do than entertain our arrogance. It's another case of subject object relations, and it's based on a faulty premise, the premise being our subjective superiority. But life isn't a territory to be conquered. It's a dance. And as any tango teacher will tell you, in that dance, the leader follows, while the follower leads.

This is perhaps the most fascinating lesson my time on this land has taught me. It isn't creation, it's *co-creation*. My imagination whirrs. Ideas bloom. I feel excited and passionate. I want to build something; a nice gazebo to sit in, for example. I believe I can. But before I so much as open the tool shed, I've learned the most crucial step in the process. I wait. I walk about the land. I listen.

We are so busy speaking and trying to etch our plans and ideas on the world at large, we have forgotten to listen. We have forgotten that life and the Earth and other people are not objects but subjects in their own right. I listen while I'm watering the vegetables. I listen when I walk aimlessly around my property. I listen in the morning and as the sun goes down. I listen at night. One of the most valuable aspects of meditation is the creation of a space in which to listen. One listens to oneself, to thoughts, to feelings, to the birds, to the wind, to that mysterious ground from where it all seems to come. One becomes sensitive and open. Synchronistic events are also a type of listening. Life is communicating with us, are we hearing her? We may return to the ways of the shaman with animals, feathers, shells, flowers – all signs marking our path.

I engage in this process of listening throughout anything I do. Is the task easy? Is it flowing? Or am I battling non-stop? Am I getting scratched or hurt or pushed away? Or am I beckoned to come closer? Is life helping or hindering me?

If the light of inspired action is behind an idea, it's the easiest most fulfilling thing in the world. If it's not? You may as well stop right now. I have learned, to my own cost and that of others, that while drive and self-belief can indeed create impressive structures, they are generally miserable and unrewarding. These are the ideologies of utopia that wreck the heaven of now. They are what most wars are being fought over, internal and external.

Want to create paradise here on Earth? Yes, think positively. If you don't believe it's even possible, it's never going to happen. Imagine it. Feel it. Have faith in it. This is crucial to manifesting anything. And then press pause. Look around. Sense whether the hand of reality is coming to meet you. Because that hand is your link to the universe, and without it you're nothing but a random blip stabbing vaguely in the direction of future pleasure. With it you're a god or goddess forging paradise right here and now.

The Nowhere

September 2014

In memory of my friend and neighbour Celal without whom The Mud wouldn't exist.

When I pick up a seed and study it, I remain baffled. No amount of theory from the field of biology ever satisfies my understanding of the seed. I invite you to study one. Really. They are often not much more than motes of dust. If you break them apart there's not much to them. From the outside or the inside, they don't really look to be secret vaults stuffed with reams of genetic data. Then you plant one. Or perhaps you didn't plant it at all, it just happened to be hunkering down in a bit of dirt. Soon, from what looks to be nothing, life sprouts. Life. Great writhing creations push forth; trees, flowers, thorn bushes, aubergine plants, bull rushes. How? Where did they come from? They came from Nowhere.

Yet just as new life burgeons, old life recoils. Again, as if into nothing. As if to Nowhere. I know it. We all know it. Earth is a restless place. Nothing upon it is still. Everything is either in a state of growth or decay. Things are bursting into creation, or they are dying. And sorry, Mother Nature, sometimes, I don't like it. Not at all.

Recently, two people dear to me died. Death is guaranteed to shake the rugs on mind's floor, and send the dust of the taken-for-granted flying. First my beautiful gran left at 94 years of age. At her funeral, my dad said, "We are all the poorer for her loss. The world is poorer." The truth of that drove home. There is often an attempt to make death palatable by talking of regeneration, of people living on in our hearts and our minds, of heavens and passing into other rooms. Yet, for those of us left here in the mud of the planet, when someone dies, something of immense value has disappeared. Into Nowhere. It is a great loss. Things have changed irrevocably. That being will never again exist, which is precisely what makes every one of us so precious.

This week another hole opened in humanity's flimsy veil of existence. The Nowhere pushed a hand through and yanked away my dear neighbour Celal. One minute he was scampering past my land calling his band of goats and sheep and dogs and cats to follow, the next he was gone. Disappeared. Just as with the seed and the sprout, I can't understand it. Where did he go? Perhaps this is what I am attempting to do here, understand this relentless wheel of change. I won't succeed of course. How could I?

I really can't talk about The Mud, or my land, or my house without including Celal. The first time I met him was at my neighbour Dudu's house. I had been on my mountain about a week. It was back in those early, dusty days of 2011 when I had no water. I was hunched over Dudu's garden tap filling a couple of bottles up and admiring her plum tree. Suddenly, an enormous Anatolian shepherd sidled round the side of her small cottage. I gulped at him. I gulped harder when he bounded over to sniff me. The dog-beast easily reached my waist. It was like being hungrily nosed by Shere Khan. On the heels of the dog, a walnut-faced little stick of a man appeared.

"Apo! Down, boy, down, down! C'mon now here's a good boy."

I looked dubiously at the man, far from convinced he had control over his hound. Apo was probably the larger, if not in height then certainly in circumference.

"Kerry, this is Celal!" Dudu crowed. She pulled her headscarf back a little and pushed Apo out of the way. "Now this is the man you're looking for. You want to cut all that grass pronto! No messing about. Get rid of it all. There'll be snakes and all sorts in there. Celal'll sort that out in a jiffy. Helps the English down the road, he does. Very trustworthy. You can leave your keys with him and never have to worry about a thing."

Celal stretched out a sinewy hand and grinned. As with many villagers the smile was littered with brown teeth and gaps. His face was a wrinkled nut topped with a tousle of grey hair. I wondered just how this curious little fellow would fare over on my camp.

I've have been lucky over and over again on this piece of earth. So lucky, I can't quite believe it at times. What did I do to deserve it? Celal was one of those strokes of immense good fortune. I understood it the first day he came to cut my grass. I am always wary about who I allow on my land, because I have tried my utmost to preserve it as a space of peace, kindness and respect for wildlife. I won't allow any sort of violence or pollution within the boundaries; including abusive language, smoking, killing or negative speaking. And I am famous for sending people off it. So it was with some trepidation I watched Celal that first morning as he sharpened the blade of his scythe.

"Please don't kill any animals," I said as I balanced my blackened two-pot Turkish kettle on the small camping stove.

"Aye, I never kill anything if I can help it. Everything has a right to live," replied Celal. He bent over to slice through the grass. He was dressed in a pair of navy beach shorts. His legs jutted from the bottoms like two thin leather straps.

After an hour or so, Celal called me over. "I only cut what's thorny and prickly. If it looked like a green plant, I left it. Did I do right?"

I stared around at the newly shorn top of my land. It was now decorated with wild green shrubs that had previously been hidden or throttled under the rampant thistle bushes. That he had meticulously saved each plant was something of a miracle in a time and place where folk are better known for jumping in a digger and ripping up anything in their path. I knew there and then; Celal was going to be my right-hand man. In the afternoon we worked side by side. He severed stalks, while I collected them into haystacks.

Of course, for all our good intention, we were still killing the grass. One being's creation is another's destruction. Nature has her rules. When the time comes, all things are sucked down into the Nowhere so that the new can rise up in their place. No one and no thing escapes. Even the lush smell of freshly cut grass is apparently a distress signal as the plant dies. No doubt Celal and I unwittingly killed ants and small bugs underfoot, too. But we tried. We did our best.

Celal possessed a sixth sense for the land and its inhabitants. In that way, he was special, and far more patient and selfless than I. I watched him carefully pick up scorpions the size of a fist with a piece of wood, and relocate them before digging. He would point out praying mantis, crickets, squirrels, birds and new plants. When he worked, he brought his troupe of animal friends with him; Apo and Ciko the dogs, Yagmur and Sahin the cats. He was the Pied Piper of the animal world with a goat and a sheep that trailed after him every day as he urged them along with '*Gel. Gel.*' The first winter when we were building my house, I would sometimes eat with him and his grown-up children in their cottage in the village. It was surrounded by ducks and chickens twittering in the yard. Celal opened the door and showed me where he slept. There was a rabbit under his bed and a bunch of kittens snuggling in it. Later he moved from the village into his wooden hut next to Dudu and me. Someone from the city or the Western world would have called it a slum or a shack. People in apartments would have pitied him. But Celal loved his handmade home and was incredibly proud of it. He built it out of old building cast-offs and parts he'd found in rubbish dumps. A new-ager might have labelled it an earthship. Sometimes the goat he named Kecibullah would clamber inside and stamp on his bed. Sometimes it climbed over the car leaving hoof marks on the bonnet. One time I saw it wander in the greenhouse and gamely nibble away all the peas. Celal's daughter-in-law shook her head in defeat. I asked her, "Why don't you shoo it out?"

"Ah. It's Dad. He won't have a bad word said about that goat."

Celal spent far more time and energy feeding his menagerie than he ever did himself. The day before he died, I saw him dragging two large olive branches over to the sheep pen before sitting down heavily and wheezing.

Nature's rules are nature's rules. Either today or tomorrow we will make way for the new. It was a sunny morning this week. Too sunny. Almost frivolously so. Dudu called me at 7 am in the morning.

"Don't be afraid. Don't be sad. I have some bad news," she stuttered.

Celal had died in his sleep of a heart attack.

Turkish rural folk deal with death very differently than those in the Western world. Death is something real and tangible, be it goats or chickens or people. It isn't locked away in old people's homes or filed out of sight by undertakers. It is a part of life. It is touched and smelt. The family carry the body of their loved one out of his home in their own hands. And they cry unabashed as they do so. I watched with stinging eyes as the village men pulled Celal out of his beloved hut in a blanket, his animals staring on. I think it was the first time I'd seen him look so at ease. I couldn't help noticing that he looked larger in death than in life – almost gigantic – while we shrunk into helpless huddles.

Ah Celal, you look so peaceful now that the concerns of the world are no longer yours. Your death is not your loss, it's ours. But let me tell you, this corner of Gaia feels the lack. An emptiness steals through the neighbourhood, gaps yawning apart where your presence once glued things together. The land creaks underfoot. She's crying your name to the sky, asking the Nowhere for answers. Something is missing. The bugs and the birds all feel it, and the trees are groaning softly in confusion. Your goat and your sheep look lost. Apo slumps in the dust. Ciko is curled in dejection. It's very quiet over here. Too quiet.

Yes, we know; the new is coming. It will blossom in the vacuum the old has left. We know; it is natural. The wild horses of change are forever charging, trampling the old underfoot to feed the seeds of the new. Yet I hope. I only hope. Will those seeds be as decent and sweet as those who at one time planted them?

Yes. Tell me. *Will* they?

Note: the Turkish letter 'c' is pronounced like an English 'j', so Celal is Jelal.

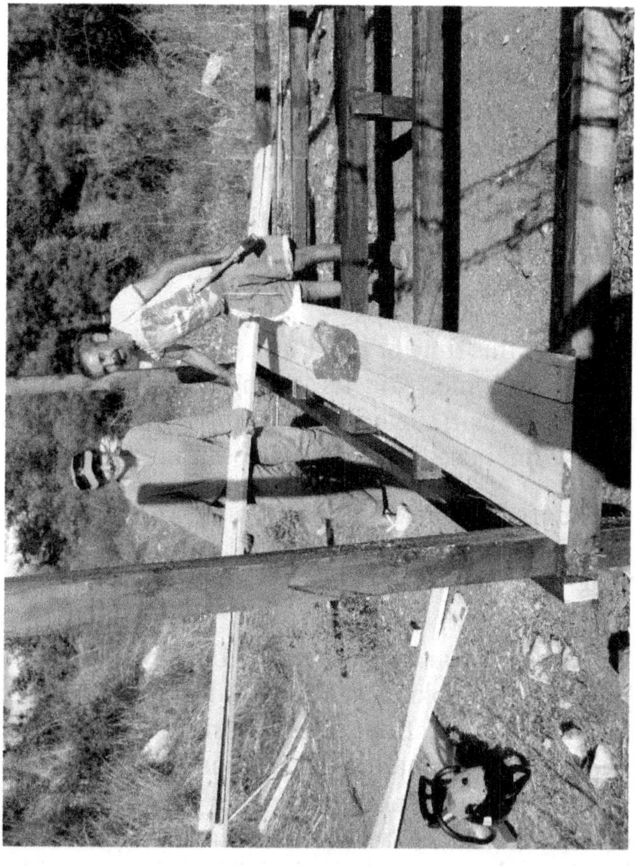

Walls

November 2014

As autumn sinks into winter, the nights on the Mediterranean turn from cool to cold. This week I watched the crooked, brown limbs of stove pipes poke out from windows, and smelt the first wafts of smoke floating out of them. It was like the mist of another world. The world of winter. Winds howl. Doors are closed. Fires are lit.

It is at this time of year that I give thanks for my cosy earthbag home. For its strength and warmth and shelter. As I sit, stove chugging, in T-shirt and leggings, I muse on those fat earth walls of mine.

Before I began natural building, I think, like most folk, I assumed the function of a wall was to protect. This isn't all that surprising. I'm issue from an education that separates the world into illusory isolated parts and has them battle it out for survival. This way of looking at the world is so pervasive, we forget it is a creation of ours derived from subjective and partial information. Separation is the window from which we Westerners observe everything; including our homes. They become our castles. The wall is a barrier to keep enemies at bay. There is an outside and an inside, and never the twain shall meet.

Yet, as I began constructing this home, I started to investigate a little more carefully into walls, and what the devil they're for. Mainstream building, unsurprisingly, follows the prevailing attitude that walls are to protect. They are built nice and strong, stuffed with insulation to keep the cold out, coated in chemicals to keep bugs and mould out. It's all about keeping stuff out.

Natural building, however, draws on nature for inspiration. What are walls for in nature? Are they all about protection, or do they serve other functions? The most obvious walls in the natural world are either the cell membranes of plants and organisms, or the skin of larger animals. Hmm, skin. How about regarding a wall as skin? I began to compare my mud bag walls to a thick earthbeast's hide.

Granted, my earthbag walls do act as a protective barrier, and a very efficient one at that. At near on half a metre thick, they can defend the interior of my house from hurricanes, rain, wild boar, bullets and fire. But it's not all about that, because life isn't all about that. Despite how we've been taught to view it, life isn't simply a power struggle, nor is it only brute strength that prevails. If it were, then this planet ought to be dominated by an Herculean iron-skinned monster with ten-foot long teeth and claws, and no sense of ethics. If it is all about strength and domination then where do daisies and butterflies and Vivaldi fit in? And obviously they do fit in, because they thrive just as well as their more brutish counterparts. Sometimes they thrive far better. Tyrannosaurus rex didn't make the cut, yet field mouse did.

Back to walls and skin. One of the most important functions of skin is sensation. Sensitivity equals an ability to respond and adapt, to transmit information from outside to inside. Sensation is the intelligence of life in its most basic form. So where does this tessellate with earthbag walls? Now, even I'll stop short at suggesting my earthbag walls experience sensation.

But what they can do is communicate information from the outside in a way a concrete wall coated in chemical paint can't. Earth, earth plaster and lime are all breathable. They allow the outside to be drawn in and the inside to flow out, yet incredibly, just like skin, they manage this feat without losing heat. So, in an earthbag house there is no mould or damp, no stagnant air. It always smells fresh and healthy, even when I've been away for two weeks. In fact, I'm always eager to inhale that first breath of Mud Home. If you add concrete anywhere in the building process, you lose this freshness. Concrete holds water. It's not permeable. It's all about protection and nothing about communication or connection.

Sound familiar?

So as winter pushes me within my ring of earth, as the doors are closed and the stove lit, I gape out of the window at the rash of stars spreading over the skin of night. Their luminescence travels light-years across galaxies until it penetrates my window pane and hits my retina. It is an information clad communication that makes me shiver. Some piece of them, albeit a reflection, has touched me. And I wonder. Really, are the stars out there at all? Or are they in here? Because we are for a moment connected. But it doesn't end there, does it. For if my mind can soar out of these earth walls and into the heavens to wonder all this, where, if anywhere, am I?

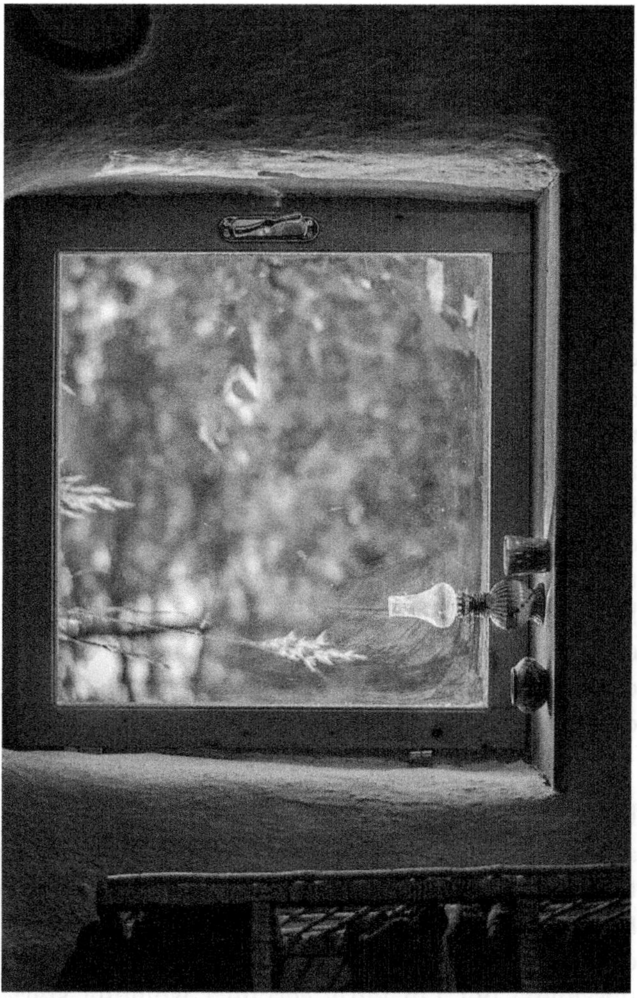

Should Everyone Move Off Grid?

December 2014

Should everyone do what I've done, jack in their job, run from the city to the hills and build an off-grid mud empire for themselves? Would it be more or less sustainable? Could humanity survive without cities? Where, after all, would we squash these ever mushrooming plagues of people? Hmm.

It is widely promulgated that without cities there simply wouldn't be enough land space for us all. Out of curiosity, I began to research a little on how much usable surface area of the planet there was for each individual. It's not easy to uncover a straight answer to that, and it depends whether the research includes the entire Earth's surface, forests, deserts or cities themselves. According to one study back in 2005 we all had a little over 5 acres of earth surface each. Huntington Funds put the figure closer to just over 1.5 acres per head. World Watch calculates it as only 0.5 acres per capita. Feeling claustrophobic yet?

There is much debate about how much land each human needs to survive. Somewhere between 5 to 10 acres is a figure that sprouts up fairly regularly, though let's be honest, far too many of these theoreticians are hypothesising from a swivel chair in a city or a suburb. I am not self-sufficient (is such a thing possible?) but I'm fairly certain I wouldn't starve if push came to shove, and I haven't even touched ¾ of my 2 acre plot. The issue isn't so much land space as what we're doing with it. Ask me to choose between 100 hectares of desert and an acre of fertile soil with a wellspring, there's no debate. I'd go for the latter. Far more crucial than metres squared, is clean water, healthy soil and healthy bio-systems, hence my ambivalence vis-à-vis cities.

When you live with your arse in the dirt, when your meals sprout primarily from your garden, when your life is dictated by the seasons and the sun rather than a Rolex, a different type of awareness evolves. The impact of everything you do to your land is obvious, and you reap what you sow very quickly. The trouble with the urban sprawl is that while it might not take up as much physical space per capita, its population is divorced from the consequences of its actions. If city folk pollute a river it doesn't impact them directly, because they can still throw a bottle of Evian in their supermarket trolley. If they waste insane amounts of energy why care as long as there is the cash to foot the bill? Why ever bother with a composting toilet? The crap is flushed away somewhere else. And therein lies the problem. A city's mess doesn't end at its asphalt fringes. If we take stock of the bigger picture, the waste, energy and water consumed by cities decimate large swathes of resources.

And yet, am I saying we should all live off-grid?

From the outside it looks as though the soundest option would be permaculture-based sustainable communities with food stuff, materials and resources shared, but...but...I'm still hesitant. There is a tendency, when folk escape from 'civilisation', to turn pristine nature into exactly that which they were running away from. Rural off-the-grid life and the world of the city are two vastly different realities, and some never adapt. Houses are generally built too big, nature's gifts are bulldozed out of existence before they are even noticed, the quiet unpeopled hours weigh heavily on those of naturally social bent, the lack of distraction bores others. City dwellers moving to the country for the first time are like refugees finding themselves in a foreign land with a language they don't speak. It takes time to adjust, and some never do. And perhaps they were never meant to.

But isn't the aim of Mud Mountain to convince everyone to join my club and be like me, build a whopping great muddy community? Isn't that what we should do?

The idea that we 'should' be doing something, is all too human. Wild cyclamen and buzzards know nothing of what they should do. They do whatever they like, can, or have to, at any given moment. So why do I write these posts? Why spend a day each month banging the keys of my laptop and spouting my earthy crap? Let it be known; I have no interest in convincing anyone to do anything, converting people is the territory of religions and dogma. Actual living is the art of the soul, and everyone does it differently.

To accept yourself, to love and believe in your talents, to follow only that which brings you joy is nature's way. Contented, self-fulfilled people generally consume less than their miserable or desensitised counterparts left with little else to do but stuff the holes inside them with noise and instant gratification (this holds true whether you live off-grid or not). The more complete you are, the more you realise the outside simply can't bring you what you most desire. It's inner peace and happiness we need more of, not just off-grid homes, because both pollution and ecology start in the mind and the heart, and just like everything else in the natural world, they grow naturally out from there.

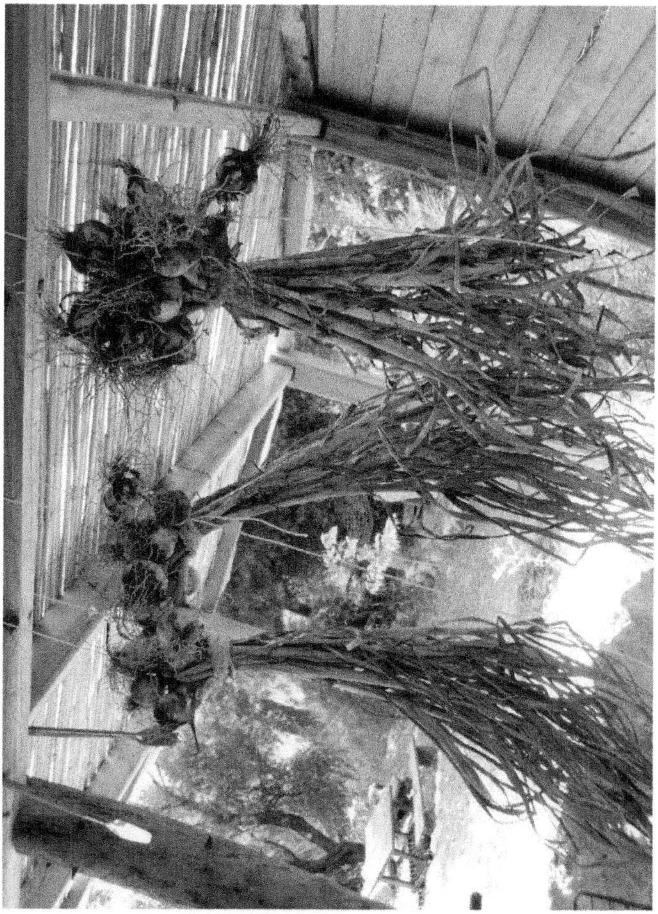

2015

Escaping the Daily Grind

January 2015

Mist rises like the smoke of inspiration, genies' clouds climbing the rock-speckled banks. The pomegranate trees are bare now. Winter has pulled off both their fruit and their leaves. Yet the olives and pines care little about winter's bullying. They are greener than ever. January's downpours have satiated their tough old roots. It's 11 am, third day of a continual deluge of rain that hasn't even let up long enough for me to visit the bathroom. When the need arises I have to don wellies, rain trousers and macintosh. Even then, I'm soaked when I return. No one is moving. Not even the shepherds. The land is a silent sponge absorbing any wisp of ambition or haste. So I have sat in my mud home for three days doing absolutely nothing constructive other than inhale the fresh aroma of my liberty.

It wasn't always like this. I've worked in the system just like most people, and the memory sits cold on my diaphragm, congealing. The sickening sound of the alarm. The bolted breakfasts. The dragging yourself to work when you are under par. The tedium and frustration of following a routine designed for someone with a very different sleep pattern, digestive system and work tempo than yours. The interminable boredom. I know I'm not alone. If you watch the popularity of the more sensible online blogs, a surprising amount chews the dream-filled cud of escaping the daily grind. There's little doubt, the driving aim of my Mud world was to eradicate the need for money and render the drudge of work obsolete. And this reminds me of something that happened two and a half years ago.

It was a full moon, September 2013. I'd just returned from a six month stint in Taiwan, the proceeds of which were supposed to keep me afloat for another year. Then I went and burned out the engine of my car (oh the metaphorical beauty of that). It wasn't really surprising as I'd filled the poor beast to the brim with roofing felt, timber, a few bags of lime, and then driven it full pelt up a mountain in mid-summer. Ahem. Now, lest you're anywhere as reckless as I am, let me tell you, burning your engine out is a very expensive business, even when your car is a twenty-year-old Turkish Fiat. If I'd been in the UK it would have been scrapped. It doesn't work like that in Turkey. To cut a long story short, the burned engine devastated my finances. I remember sitting with the late Celal under my grandmother olive tree and bawling. The thought of going back to that; to work, to punch-in-clocks, to doing a job I'd long fallen out of love with, well, it felt like I was on death row.

"You know what?" I said to Celal. He was sitting on a stool in the shade and staring out at the view and chewing on a twig.

"What?"

"I think I might rob a bank. I mean let's face it, if I get caught the worst that will happen is I'll get three years in jail. Come to think of it, I wouldn't even have to cook. What a bonus! I could just sit and write all day."

Celal grinned.

"Aye," he said. 'There ain't never been no point in doing an honest day's work. Look at the rich, they're all robbers anyway."

But I was only half listening, because I was suddenly imagining doing a stint in a Turkish jail. We are no longer in the era of *Midnight Express*. How bad could it be? I came to the conclusion the food would be OK, because the Turks never serve junk food wherever you are. And who'd be in there with me? Badass Turkish women who'd murdered their abusive husbands, and left-wing political dissidents. The more I thought about it, the more attractive jail time was looking. Heating paid for. Warm showers. It surely couldn't be much worse than being chewed up by the teeth of The Machine's cogs for another year.

I exhaled a very long slow yogic breath. Now, what state have we reached when an educated quad-lingual forty-year-old woman considers jail time preferable to a job? The longer I thought about it, the more unreasonable it all seemed. I swear, the only reason I didn't undertake a robbery was a sense of ethics and the vague threat of bad karma. I know not everyone hates their job, and good for those that are happy. Yet for the millions throughout the world who work in factories, fill supermarket shelves, populate the tight rectangles of cubicle land, are bullied by their work peers or, like me, whose hearts cry out to do something they love, The Job is prison.

It was the loathing of The Job that drove me to sell my car, to begin building using scraps, to start learning to survive on next to nothing. It became something of a game. *How long can I keep this up?* I wondered. Initially I worried about things like; What happens when I get sick? I don't have health insurance. But I was hardly ever ill. When you live according to nature's rhythms, if you sleep when you're tired and get up when you're awake, when you eat properly and rest properly and feel blessed to be alive, illness flees from you like an energy corporation from an environmental lobby. As one of my friends in the valley put it, "It's nuts, people are stressed out working to pay their health insurance which makes them sick. Why not cut out the middle man?"

Yes, it's scary to leave a salary behind and not know where the next buck is coming from, but the wide space that opens up in place of The Job allows hefty gusts of creative power to enter. We are so much more resourceful than we have been taught to think. And life can be so much more benevolent too.

Two and a half years on and I've never been back to work again. Oh thank The Mud and the rain for that! I'm no longer a slave but a free woman. Let me say this; now I've tasted the sweet nectar of liberty, there's no going back to the grind. Yes The Job really is prison, and no you don't have to remain in it.

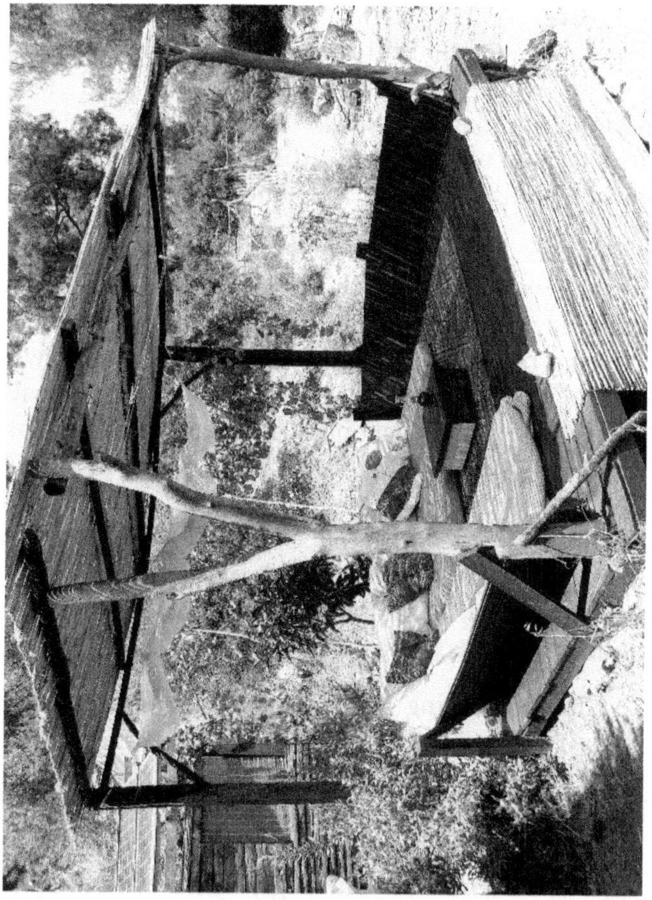

Coming Home

February 2015

For the first time in three years, I left The Mud for a longer while and travelled to that well known Indonesian paradise, Bali. Before I left, one of my friends said of the place, "I thought Sri Lanka was the most beautiful place on the planet, and then I saw Bali."

It *was* beautiful, with its thin snakes of broken tarmac writhing through the green, valleys contoured with rice paddies, bamboo architecture, flower-filled offering boxes littering the paths. As with everywhere nowadays, a traveller has to scavenge for hideouts from the oily, red belly of mass tourism. But it was still beautiful. Beautiful to feel the heat on my skin in February, to dive with manta rays, beautiful to eat tofu, beautiful to smell difference, to be transported from a life of familiars to the wilderness of the hitherto unknown. Slowly, I shed my earthy layers until I was almost Mudless.

I love travelling for many reasons. One of them is that it rips The Self out its context and plants it somewhere new. It offers the opportunity to glance over your shoulder at your world back home and view it from ten steps removed. Without our houses, our jobs, our friends and our dogs, which can at any time be taken from us, who and what are we? Who was I without The Mud?

There was a time when I loved my land so intensely, I actually thought I couldn't live without it. It was my best friend, and I felt a visceral need to be connected to it. Perhaps this is the same with all love affairs. In the beginning we lose ourselves in the union, which allows it to transform us and thus we evolve. But over time – unless we become addicted to the rush which tends to bring about a more cataclysmic end to the relationship – the bond relaxes. We find we can enjoy our time to ourselves as much as our time with our lovers. We appreciate them through togetherness and separation in equal measure.

In Bali, I enjoyed simply sitting with my soul and hearing it speak, hearing the whispers and callings that were beyond The Mud, feeling my imagination roam in new directions and allowing the fingers of Another Place to leave her prints on me. Soon The Mud receded almost out of view. Then it was time to return.

Returns can often be difficult; the soul is still in the old, while the senses have arrived in the new. The first impression of home is informative because of this. It is a virgin wall uncoloured by the ideas, emotions and memories we will soon tack over it. It takes a couple of days to 'settle in', for the soul to return and plaster the walls of now with its associations. In this small temporal gap, we have the chance to see our homes momentarily devoid of ourselves.

The day I returned, I walked down my path, already overgrown after just less than a month. My dog stopped maddeningly often to smell this rock and that stick, trying to catch up on what she'd missed. The slope was covered in a lush green down. My leeks and onions were lost in a mesh of burgeoning grass. But it was the mountains that forced me to pause. Their massive grey heads formed a circle around me. They held an exquisite view in their forested arms, and then let it slide between them into the sea. The sky seemed to go on forever, the blue rising higher and higher. The hairs on my arms bristled. I was transfixed.

Next, I walked over to my little house of Mud. I smiled and dropped my backpack on a kitchen chair. Sliding my key in the lock, I pushed the door. It opened onto a rustic, nobbled world of Turkish carpets, bookshelves and mud sculptures. There were little alcoves and pretty mosaics, painted stones and glass beads set in plaster. I gasped at the sight of it. 'Oh my God!' I said to myself. 'What a lovely little house! Who could have made it?' It was strange. I saw nothing of the cracks that needed filling, nor the boards needing a new coat of oil, nor the dust collecting in the corners. All the 'faults' that I normally bothered myself with, had mysteriously vanished.

I kicked off my boots and stepped inside. The smell of the juniper floor was dizzying. The air cool and fresh. As I ran my eyes over the bumpy walls, they oozed with spirit and warmth. Jumping onto a *kilim* cushion, I let my Mud home hold me as I stared out at the view.

I shook my head. I was just as besotted as ever.

Sorry Bali, *this* is beautiful, I thought. Yup. There ain't no place like home.

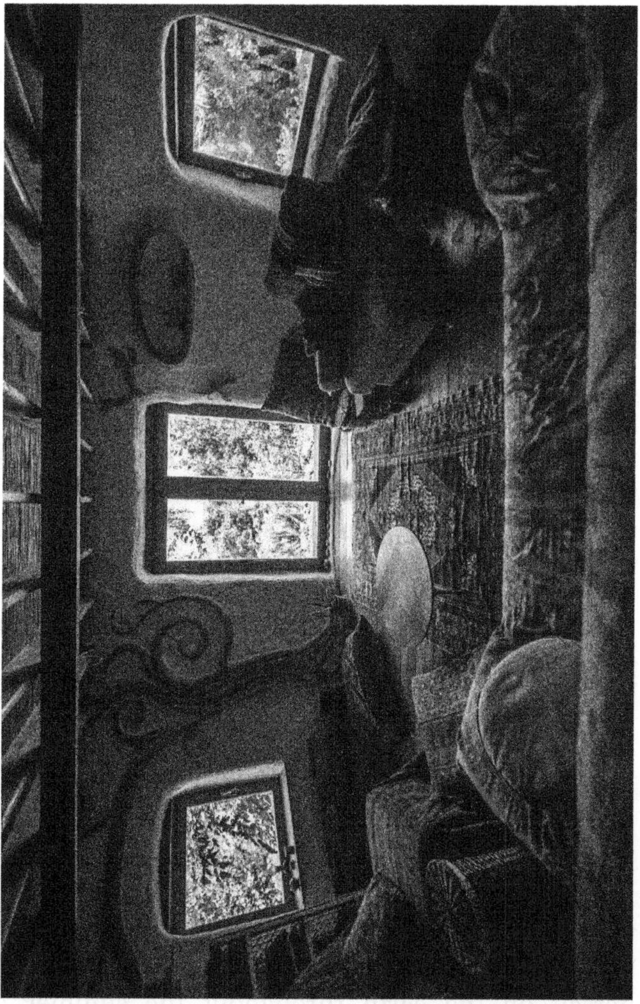

Listening to your Land

March 2015

You've heard me waffle on about listening to your land. No doubt you're sick of it. People write to tell me they're planning to build a natural home off-grid, and ask me for advice. Merrily I tap into the email: You need to listen to your land. But what am I talking about when I say that? And how does that relate to you?

You can read all about my personal experience of listening to my land in the first and second Mud Mountain blog posts I ever wrote. I was starry eyed and fresh from the system when I first set up camp here with little more than a tent, pick, spade and a wheelbarrow. This enchanting rectangle of the Earth wriggled under my skin and set me alight. It changed me. And I changed it.

Here's another more recent example of how communicating with your land can powerfully impact building decisions. This time the off-gridder is Ayşe, hiking star of my biographical novel *Ayşe's Trail*. We bought our plots the same year and in the same area.

Last May, after a foray into adult education in Istanbul, Ayşe finally moved onto her virgin space. Like me she took little more than a tent (though there are tents and then there are *tents*. Let's just say hers wasn't a fifty dollar Carrefour cheapie). Like me, she staked herself on the earth throughout the summer and developed a loving relationship with her domain. She cleared spaces, built walls, set up an outside kitchen and shower area, hammered together a composting toilet. Like me, she had no power and no running water. Initially, she planned to procure a government connection, but for legal reasons was unable to.

It was July when I visited her. The sun was cutting incandescent paths through the forest above and scorching the ground it hit. We sat on a rug she'd laid under a pine. Pouring me a mug of tea, she sighed. She was demoralised.

"I've made a decision, Kerry. I just can't do this without water. It's too difficult. Either I find a wellspring on this land, or I'm giving up."

I nodded understandingly. My two years of life without running water were challenging to say the least. It's the one and only thing you really do need.

"What do you feel the land has to say?" I asked.

She shrugged. "I don't know. I love it here, I just love it. But I can't make it without water. If this place wants me, I guess it will give it to me. If not, I'm going."

"Have you any ideas where water might be?" I sipped my tea and gazed over her plot. It was buzzing with life. West facing, the slope was crammed full of ancient olive trees and towering pines. Some had collapsed from old age, their twisted carcasses providing her with ample firewood and building materials. To me, it felt congenial and welcoming.

"Well there are some blackberries over there," she said.

I looked up. Just above us was a small gulch filled with brambles. It was the kind of detail you had to be living on the land a while to notice. Had she simply paid a digger to flatten the site at the outset, they would have been lost. In mid-July, it was unthinkable that blackberries could be surviving without water. I'd made three attempts at growing blackberries, only to watch them die of thirst every summer no matter how much I tried to water them. This looked hopeful at any rate.

Digging for a wellspring is a nail-biting endeavour. Every metre you mine is costing you, and there's no guarantee you will find your liquid gold. People have been known to dig a hundred metres and remain empty handed. Underground water is frustratingly elusive, with streams changing course at the drop of a hat. So when the day came and the digger rolled onto the bottom corner of Ayşe's land, she was tense. It was make or break.

The machine took a couple of swipes at the earth, then a couple more. It was no more than two metres down before water began not just dribbling but gushing out. This is the stuff of off-grid fantasy, I can tell you. A concrete ring was installed, and a small pump attached. Ayşe was back in business.

That wasn't all, however. Once the water issue was resolved, Ayşe also wanted to build a mud home. Being of pioneer spirit herself, she wanted to forge something new; an alternative technique for natural adobe. She had a feeling about where she wanted her house. Then she asked my opinion.

"Ah Ayşe, if you feel it should be over in that little secluded corner, then follow your gut," I said. "I don't really like giving advice on other people's land because there are few rules, and logic so often just doesn't come up with the goods."

"Yes, but I'm asking for your idea because you've some experience."

"Well," I said. "Logically speaking, if you think about where the sun is rising and setting, and where it rises and sets in winter, that spot you've pointed to could be dark and cold."

Ayşe furrowed her brow. Then I pointed to another corner. We both agreed this space saw plenty of sun in winter, but received ample afternoon shade in summer. Still, I was uncomfortable. "But hey, maybe there's a reason you warmed to that other spot that we don't know about yet. Maybe the land was urging you there. Who knows?" I said.

Who knows indeed? Unfortunately, Ayşe listened to me and logic, and placed her home in the lower east side of the land. She hammered together a wooden frame for her mud home from repurposed palettes, and began the slow process of filling it with an adobe concoction. She worked with one other person for a month, before deciding to complete the house single-handedly. Then something happened. A family who owned the neighbouring land, and who hadn't been seen for over two years, abruptly returned. They moved into a small bungalow directly below Ayşe's new mud house. It irritated Ayşe, who like me was looking for solitude. Then the rains came early. It slowed Ayşe's progress to a halt. By late October her walls were only a third complete. She wasn't going to make it before winter.

In the end, Ayşe had to commission the building of a small wooden bungalow to shelter her through the winter. And guess where that hut was built? On the original spot she had liked from the outset. How happy she was as she trotted up and down the wooden steps hidden by the bristling pines from all and sundry.

So the moral of the story is don't listen to me, or your neighbour, or the architect, or any amalgam of logical ideas. Listen to your land. Because it's between you and her. Who knows what secrets she's storing? Ultimately only she can show you the way.

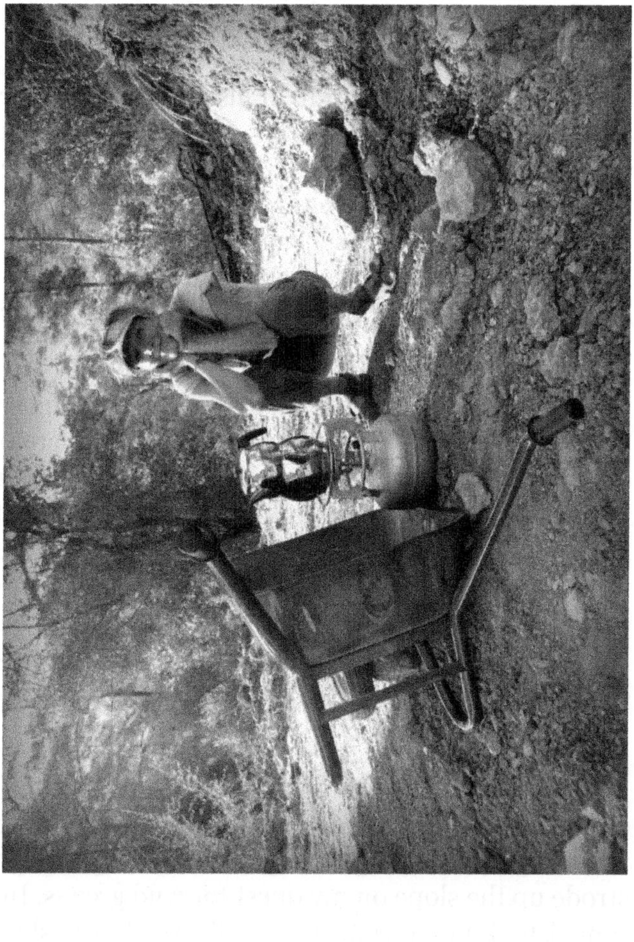

In Completion

May 2015

Every morning when I step out of my mud home, Rotty the dog hustling about my lower legs, my eyes fall to the back step. This is often because I have just tripped and wrung my ankle. It might also be because there is a swamp the other side of my door and I'm going to need wellington boots to wade through it. You see it isn't a back step. It's a clutter of rocks strewn at the edge of a strip of hardened earth that is supposed to be my back step. I just haven't got round to finishing it yet. It has been languishing in this state of incompletion for about three years now.

It must have been two months ago I gave myself a bit of a talking to. Enough! said the dictatorial quadrant of my personality to the indolent dreamer. I'm sick of looking at this damn wreck of a step. Just do it for God's sake! So I hauled myself up by the wellie tops, averted my eyes from the one thousand and one other jobs itching to yank me away from the task in hand, and conjured up an idea of how that back step could be. Pulling a rusty old oil tin from the shed, I began collecting rocks.

Two pails were filled. I deposited the stones at the edges of where my up and coming step was to be. I now felt hungry. Grabbing a large Turkish yoghurt pot, I strode up the slope on my quest for wild greens. In the time it took me to collect a meal's worth, the sky had thickened with clouds. They bubbled and boiled about the hill, a cabal of meteorological grumpiness. I returned to my kitchen. The greens hadn't even made it into the pan before the sky collapsed into an onslaught of rain. It lasted about five days.

That was the last time I tried to complete the back step. Now I trip over the rocks I collected instead.

The step is one of many examples of incompletion littering the bumpy terrain of The Mud. There's the kitchen floor, which one day I'll cover in slabs so that I can wash up without rocky lumps sticking into my boots. There's the mayhem of broken tiles heaped about the wooden table under the olive tree. They are waiting to become a wonderful mosaic. They've been waiting at least two years. There's the summer gazebo with three back rests out of five completed. Even the vegetable terrace extends just as far as the string beans, after which the rocky wall peters out mid curve.

Sometimes I wonder why I don't simply plough on to the end of one job before taking on another. I have my reasons. If I dig a little deeper into the mud of my psyche and excavate a few fears and desires, I find a terror of completion. Because to reach a Mud Conclusion would be like death. I don't want my creation to end. I love it. Thus I leave loose ends flapping all over the place. Untied. Unresolved.

But what am I afraid of? The weather and the seasons roll on regardless of my unease. As I sit here watching spring pull winter apart at the seams, scattering my land with clover and vetch, and the sky with clouds of swallows, it's obvious. The revolution of the planet drags us breathlessly from old to new, and will do so until it stops turning. It's relentless. Completion isn't coming. There is no end. There are only pauses and movement, lulls and change. And none of it is ever what we expect.

Yet sometimes, when I sit quiet, legs crossed, eyes closed, and move from outside to inside, I find Another Place. It's silent and deep and vast. From there it looks different. The human striving for a finished product is based on the idea that the future is somehow more complete than the present, that there is a state nearer to perfection ahead. But from the eye of the cyclone, the ever-evolving dynamic of life seems perfectly in completion right now. It's not a static object. It's an all-encompassing land. A place where every stage of growth and decay has its rightful place in the whole. Occasionally, on good days, I get it. This is Completion. And I'm in it.

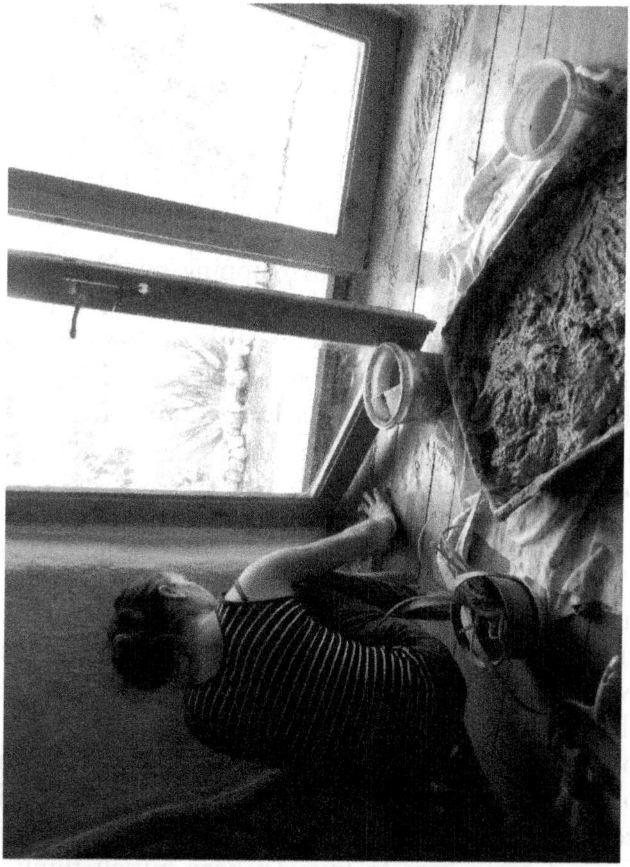

It Just Happens

June 2015

"I've no idea how you do it; build a house, manage a garden, write books, keep a blog going. Where do you find the time?"

You know what? I've no idea how it happens either. It's utterly incomprehensible now I look at it.

As I sit here (it's 11 am) supping my filter coffee, listening to the crickets whirring deliriously and watching the olives sway in the breeze, the light skipping blithely from leaf to leaf, it gives me pause to think. Time is a mercurial variable. Effort likewise. And neither appear to have anything to do with productivity. How peculiar!

I suppose from the outside it must look as though I'm some sort of maniac; all these creations popping up here, there and everywhere like oily, pink tourists in summer. And there's just this one woman on a hill, with a hammer in one hand and a computer mouse in the other. It evokes the image either of some weather-beaten, crazed old hag running herself into the ground, or an achievement-obsessed superwoman. But I didn't come here to achieve. That was what I was running from. I came here to live. To hear myself think. To stretch the hands of my soul into the deepest pockets of my being and ponder on what comes out.

As far as things 'happening' is concerned, from the inside it all seems to move incredibly slowly. Sometimes I'm rather impatient with the pace. Yet when I stop and tally it up, I receive a different impression, one I'm thankfully reminded of by the outside world when it asks "how do you do all that?" In the past month, in ways I really don't grasp, *Mud Ball* has been published, The Mud free earthbag building PDF has been written, my blog has been updated, the gazebo back rests have been hammered in place, the kitchen floor has been dug ready for tiles, a new wooden kitchen table has been made, the garden has been weeded (again and again), the beans and the tomatoes have been strung up, a succulent garden created, the summer bathroom has been cleared, the summer composting toilet emptied and ready for use, the hammocks hung up...Honestly, I have no idea how these things happened. How? *How*?

The only thing that hasn't happened is the back step. It's still a mess. Its time hasn't come.

Now if I told you that I spend a good half of my day mooching about just thinking, that during the summer I drive to the beach most afternoons and swim before reclining in a café to read a book, that I meditate at least an hour a day and swing in my hammock each evening engaging in nothing more strenuous than a good mulling on life, love and the universe, that I never really feel busy (except in the month of April when the garden can turn a little berserk), what will you say? What will I say, come to that?

I tell you, I am not busy. It's not really possible to be busy in Turkey. Neither the earth nor the culture allow it. Even a trip to buy a mosquito net can have you supping tea for an hour. Alright, I'm not lazy either. I don't spend entire weekends prostrate in front of the television, the only visible movement of my body being the twitching of my arm as my hand forages for crisps.

I'm active. I'm alive. But workwise, I probably spend about an hour a day writing, and about two hours in the garden. So that's an extremely undemanding three-hour day I'm 'grafting'.

That's it. I generally just do what I feel like, when I feel like it. And perhaps that's the key. We Westerners have been drip-fed a terrible lie that busyness is productive, that by running around like headless chickens we're somehow being useful, that the faster we drive the more we achieve, that forcing issues resolves them more quickly. Yet, as I stare out into the wilderness beyond, I notice creativity blooms in the gaps. It is nurtured in the silences. We've got it the wrong way round. We think we will do do do, and then stop for a break and admire our workmanship, when in fact the break is apparently required before we act, because it's the non-doing that begets the doing not vice versa. Yes, I see. Butterflies don't flap their rainbow wings before they've enjoyed a good slothful stint in a chrysalis, trees don't push new branches into the sky before they've snoozed nice and peacefully for a winter, shoots don't even entertain the notion of sprouting until they've sat resolutely still in a seed pod for months. Snakes and mice spend half their life sleeping. I'm watching nature. She takes plenty of time out. And few are more creative than her.

I ran from the system to avoid busyness. It was a flee from stress, from the never-ending chase after a few meaningless rungs on a status ladder that so obviously count for nothing. So I've pitted myself against the rush. I refuse to participate in it. If anything is supposed to get done, it will. If it's not, it won't. And yet, as you see, it happens. Books get written, blogs get updated, gardens are dug, flowers burgeon. It just happens. And now I look at it, though I understand not how, there seems to be a lot of it happening too.

When Gaia Puts her Foot Down

July 2015

Sometimes I wonder whether I make it all up. Does my land really communicate with me? Is there anything outside myself with which to engage in exchange? A little scepticism is always healthy. Back in the 18th century, the ultimate sceptic David Hume argued: "Objects have no discoverable connexion together; nor is it from any other principle but custom operating upon the imagination, that we can draw any inference from the appearance of the one to the existence of the other."

Hume pointed out something crucial. Just because we see two things occur in sequence again and again, doesn't necessarily mean one caused the other. In one paragraph all hope is dashed. I'm making it all up.

And then, out of the blue, something untoward happens between me and my land; a coincidence so peculiar or outrageous, I struggle to remain sceptical in the face of it. So I shall relate my latest Mud tale and let you decide. Did my land communicate with me? Or am I just imagining a causal relationship?

Winter was long this year, and it dug cold, wet trenches into spring. Spring became waterlogged and thus waded through the months in pursuit of warmer climes. Even in June, nights slid down to a chilly fifteen degrees rendering sleeping outside unpleasant. As a result, just like the reptiles, I was slow leaving my nest. The outside remained out. The wilderness seemed to retreat from me. I've been sensing it retreat further and further every year.

Initially, I mourned the loss of my Eden; the first grazes of the wild, the first breaking apart of my 'civilised' shell, and those early conversations with my land. This year a cooler wave of acceptance began to slosh over me. Change is inevitable, I sighed. Perhaps the loss of the intimacy I first experienced here was to be replaced by growth and experience.

And then again perhaps not.

It couldn't have been more than a month ago. The sun finally struck a decent ray over my hill. A pair of agama lizards raised their dragon heads on my rock garden, and I could hear tortoises rustling in leaves. Summer was timorously making her move. So I stepped out of my mud home. For the umpteenth time I ignored the heap of rubble that is still my back step, and walked toward Grandmother Olive. Rotty the Dog lazily poked her head out of her kennel eyeing my direction. I was holding a tablet and headphones in one hand and a cushion in the other. For the first time this season I had decided to indulge in a bit of hammock swinging.

My hammock is tethered to Grandmother Olive. This is where I recline, usually at dusk, with the express intention of listening to my land. It was only 11 am, and the area was still draped in a leaf-dappled shade. I said I was clutching headphones. Now, I listen to music in my house. I'll listen to it in my gazebo too. But I never listen to music in that hammock. Ever. That area has always been special for me; a magical point of exchange between me and nature.

As I said, the wilderness was receding. Things were changing. I was changing. I slung the cushion onto the web of rope. Then I slid on my headphones and lowered myself into the mesh cocoon. Fiddling with the settings of the tablet, I glanced up at Grandmother Olive. The thought loomed in my mind. I never do this. This is my place to listen to my land. I wonder if this is OK? Batting the question from my mind, I gamely pressed the play button.

I was a little over a minute into the first song. Just one minute. One minute into the first time I had ever brought technology onto that hammock. One minute since posing the question. I had just shut out my home and the wildlife around it and was lost in another electronic world, when Rotty began barking wildly. I turned to face her, irritated that she was disrupting my reverie. What now? I fumed. My vexation turned to perturbation. Rotty was barking at me. And it was the type of barking she reserved for wild boar, cats and rather irrationally tall, blonde females.

I yanked off my headphones and stared at my hysterical dog, hackles raised on her shoulders in a row of furry spikes. "Rotty, what the hell is up with you?" I shouted. Then I noticed she wasn't actually barking at me, but a little below me, just under my hammock. I turned and looked down, half-expecting to see a Swedish long jumper.

It was my turn to feel my hackles rise.

There, curled into the crux of Grandmother Olive's trunk, fangs glistening, head raised and ready to lunge was a one-and-a-half metre long, five-centimetre-thick black snake. It was squiggled up about seventy centimetres from the back of where my neck had been.

We were now facing each other off with nowt but the hammock strings between us.

I'm used to snakes. Once upon a time I was terrified of them, but through familiarity my fear has evaporated. Snakes look disconcerting but are basically shy, harmless creatures that will slope away at the first opportunity. I've seen plenty of them, and they are always moving in the opposite direction, as fast as they can muster. I have never in all my eighteen years of living in Turkey seen a snake raise itself up ready to lunge. I had never until that moment seen a snake's fangs close up. I've never before felt the visceral and powerful life force they represent as they coil up like springs, open their huge mouths and hiss.

Did I mention it was about seventy centimetres from the back of my neck?

Adrenalin is amazing stuff. I vaulted out of that hammock and found myself at least three metres from it. Then I dragged back my heroic Rotty, who was waging an impressively loyal 'one for all' barking attack upon Snake. Snake, seeing a window of escape, slid out from Grandmother Olive's trunk. The last I saw of it was a thick, black cable burning a trail to Dudu's land.

Heart pounding, I ran to the house. I opened the door and hurled the tablet onto my sofa. The close up image of Snake rearing, fangs bared, ready to kill, seared an impression on my mind like a psychic branding iron. It was terrifying, and it took me a good half an hour to calm down.

But calm down I did. Soon, I stepped out of the house again, and tentatively made my way over to Grandmother Olive. Shuddering, I looked up and down her thick sinewy trunk. Her strong sculpted arms bore the magnificent designs of mature bark. Grandmother Olive must be at least sixty, but she's in great shape. She stood there like empress of the whole damn world. She bristled. I lowered my head guiltily.

"OK, OK I get the message!" I muttered.

A light breeze picked up. She rustled her leaves.

I won't be listening to music in that hammock again. I'll be listening to Grandmother Olive. Hume could be right of course*. Perhaps it was simply one event following another, and me perceiving causality between the two. But these things happen so often, it beggars belief. At some point you have to be sceptical about scepticism.

I'm sceptical. Very sceptical.

Following Grandmother Olive's clip round the ear, I have made a concerted effort to reconnect with the outside this summer. I completed my gazebo and sleep once more within an Aladdin's cave of stars. I've recreated my outside bathroom, so I now shower upon an open-air rock feeling like Eve in the Garden again. My forest reading room has been refurbished with the pines, oaks and crickets weaving it into a hive of creative thought. The spirits of the wild are creeping out once more. And they're whispering new secrets I want to hear.

Hume, one of my favourite philosophers, was a true sceptic (as opposed to the posse of pseudo sceptics about today who pick and choose when to be sceptical). He argued that just because you've seen B follow A a thousand times, doesn't prove that B will follow A on the 1001st occasion. He would have made the same claim of gravity, and indeed his philosophy basically created a dead-end in purist empirical theory. The point of his philosophy was to show that we don't actually know anything, and all claim to knowing is little more than belief. "When I am convinced of any principle, 'tis only an idea, which strikes more strongly upon me. When I give preference to one set of arguments above another, I do nothing but decide from my feeling concerning the superiority of their influence."

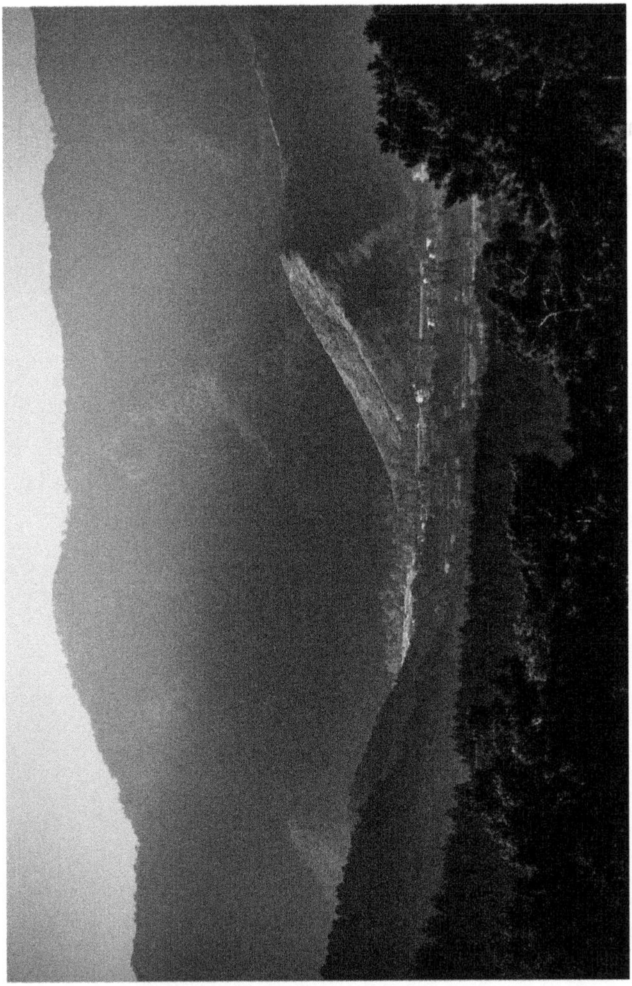

The Secret Garden

August 2015

Until now I haven't done much to publicise The Mud site. I've let it grow organically, and it has wriggled its way upwards in gentle anfractuous pulses, a bit like the wild grapevine outside my bathroom. This is the same grapevine that was dismissed by both Dudu and Celal as being a waste of space, because it was wild and would never bear fruit. Today that same vine is bulging with sweet, globules of purple. Well it would. It's next to my composting toilet.

Back to The Mud. This spring, I decided it was make or break time for www.themudhome.com. The site has germinated, it has pushed its virtual head through the soil, grown leaves and branches, and a fairly stout trunk. But it's time for it to bear a little fruit too. Lord knows, I've watered it enough. So I took inspiration from the grapevine. Last month I decided to throw a little manure on. Flippin' 'eck! As we say back home.

The Mud website has burgeoned. And naturally, all sorts of other life is attracted. I'm blessed with flocks of happy emails, the buzzings of would-be natural builders and freedom seekers all greeting me from far and near. It's a good feeling to see the fruit you planted enjoyed by others, to hear people say they had never considered building without cement until they saw your house, to have your books and posts devoured like succulent grapes, to connect with like-minded souls. I had no idea there were so many!

Quite naturally too, those in the vicinity would like to visit, to see The Mud in the flesh. It pains me to turn Mud searchers down, it really does. I have been delving into nooks of my mind this month, trying to feel out just why I can't have visitors. Then something happened. And I got it. I really got it.

I was clearing out my shed a few weeks ago when I came across a box full of books. I pulled apart the floppy cardboard flaps, and there on the top was the well-known children's story, *The Secret Garden* by Frances Hodgson Burnett. Pulling it out, I read the first page, and couldn't put it down.

Just in case you haven't read it, *The Secret Garden* concerns a contrary little girl (horrid even) called Mary Lennox who has been orphaned in India. Mary is shipped back to Yorkshire to live in a dark manor house with a hunchback uncle, his sick child called Colin, and a locked secret garden. What more could she want, eh? To cut a long story short, Mary sniffs out the key to the secret garden and breaks in. She begins tending the crocuses and messing about in the earth which is full of Magic. Yet the garden remains a secret. (Shh!) Eventually she tells Dickon, a local boy who has a way with animals and possesses a bit of Magic himself. The two children attempt to bring the garden back to life, and the therapeutic effect of the endeavour renders Mary much less horrid than she was. Eventually, she also lets sick Colin into the secret. Both of them are healed by the secret garden. Colin even begins walking.

Naturally, I was enthralled by the tale because it mirrored so closely my own experience here on the land; the healing properties of tending the earth, the connection with animals, the Magic. Yet most significant of all, the story highlighted a point I'd unwittingly passed over in my own experience. The importance of the secret element in the garden. How primal it must be for each of us to have a space of our own, a place outside eyes can't pierce, a corner of the Earth we can be explore our souls, and damn it, do what the hell we like!

This need is incredibly universal. Even my dog doesn't want to share her kennel, and sniffs at me irritably when I try to get in it. (Now, you may rightly ask why I was trying to get in my dog's kennel in the first place. Honestly, I just wondered what she'd do.) Children make dens, husbands construct man caves, authors hide away in purpose-built writing rooms, Celal had his wooden hut, my granddad had a garden shed in which he'd sit upon an upturned bucket.

We all harbour this yearning for privacy, because society is officious, judgemental and staid. It's like a nagging parent, or a bossy warden, incessantly restricting the expression of our true selves. We need a secret garden where we can play without the outside world interfering. For some it might be about the freedom to chuck motorbike parts all over the carpet, for others it could be about not having to make cup of tea for anyone, or not having to wax your legs, for others it might be about making love unabashed in the forest on a whim, or watering the plants naked, for others it could be a space where the phone never rings, or the boss can't bother you, perhaps it's a child's cubby hole in which you create a magic world, a safe place where adults can't ridicule your imagination.

The Mud is no different. While I have willingly published a virtual window into my world, The Mud reality must remain in the dark, because this is my own private playground. And I get it. It's the secrecy which allows my creativity to roam. It's the intimacy of the place which brings me and it alive. If The Mud became public, it would kill it. I would run a mile, pull down my site, and probably never write another thing.

So, Mud friends, enjoy the fruits my secret garden pushes forth. Take what you want of them. I'm pretty generous with my free information, I think. But sorry, the garden will remain locked. Concealed. Unseen. It must. Or it will die.

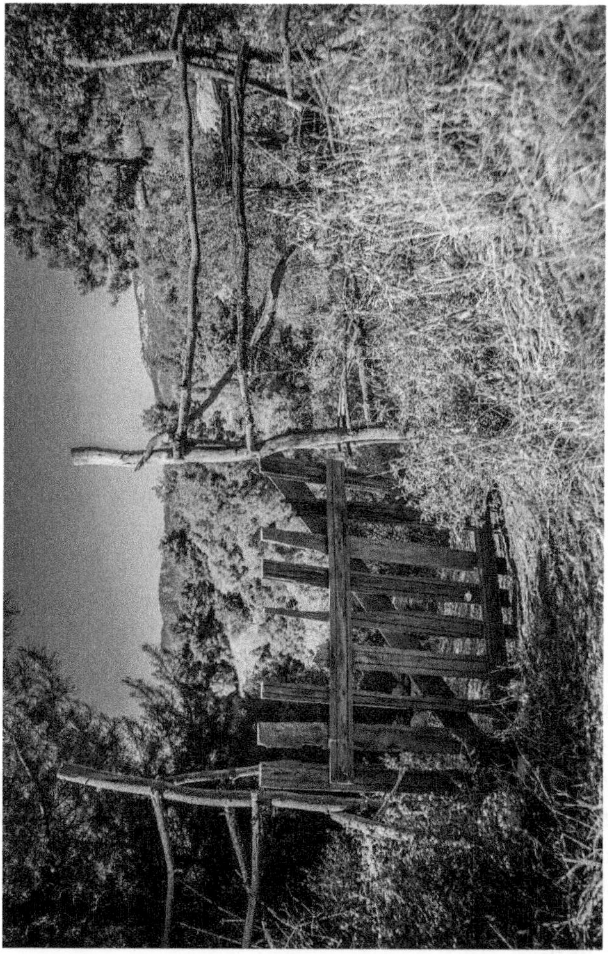

The Wisdom Carob Speaks

October 2015

The carob is one of nature's less illustrious confections. Unlike honey, the carob doesn't look much; a hard brown pod, warped, dry and on superficial examination, disappointingly ungooey. The locals call carobs *keçi boyunuzu* or goat's horns. But looks often deceive. The carob is the treacle of life. It is virility and life force in seed form. When crushed and boiled for hours in a cauldron, thick black molasses are formed; this dark elixir is endowed with all sorts of powers; it boosts immune systems, enriches haemoglobin and sends libidos rocketing to Mars.

Carob trees are two a penny in my neighbourhood. But there's a special one. A secret one. One I haven't told anyone about. Until now. Rotty, Apo and I pass her on our walk each morning. She's an incredible carob tree. Probably a good 60–80 years old. I call her the Wisdom Carob, and I climb into her ample arms whenever I have a difficult question to ask. Well, she's seen a lot that carob has. Her eyes run long and far through her wood. An enormous umbrella of boughs sprout from her multiple trunks. In summer she's a leaf-spattered dome of shade spanning about twelve metres in diameter. Well, she was...

Sigh.

Every moment, the Old is leaving and the New is arriving. Just recently I've been hearing the New knocking, albeit timorously, at the door of my own soul. Only I've not known quite how to let it in, or even if I want to. I've been in decent places before only to throw them away for 'a dream' which inevitably became a nightmare. I have no dream now though. No idea of how I could better the Now. Yet I know I've filled the container of the Old to the brim, to the point it's overflowing. There's a surplus of joy and wonder and life. But there's also a great unknowing. When you feel complete, where do you aim for next? Is there any point aiming?

So a few days ago, I walked to the Wisdom Carob. Her massive woody hand reached out of the earth and plucked at the warm autumn air. I climbed between two of her trunk fingers and sat for a while, back cradled by those huge boughs, legs swinging. I let my dilemma float from me. It wafted through the branches and swirled between the evergreen leaves. The sound of an accordion drifted hauntingly up the valley. I shivered. The sky darkened momentarily. Gusts of wind agitated the carpet of dead leaves below the carob's canopy. Then Wisdom Carob spoke.

"You have to let go of everything for the New to have a chance," she said. "The past, the images in your head. Let go of prejudices and dreams. All of it. Everything. Every preconceived notion you have about what the New could be. Because the New simply isn't the Old."

Urgh. I hopped down and mooched back to my land. I didn't have the slightest intention of letting go of everything. I mean I don't mind letting go of a bit here and there. But *everything*? I wouldn't know how to even if I tried.

The very next day I headed for the city to visit a friend. I stayed overnight and the next morning indulged in a sound therapy session. My friend randomly picked an oil to work with. It was chamomile. Turning the page of her oil book, she read aloud, "German chamomile promotes a letting go of the old and stale, so that the fresh and new can evolve..."

I closed my eyes and groaned. I'd be lying if I said these coincidences surprise me anymore. They happen every day.

The following afternoon I returned to the sun stroked folds of the valley, stopping by at Dudu's house to drop off some bread. Dudu sat on her sofa, her brown green headscarf slipping off her silver hair. She was rocking a new born baby to sleep, the grandson of the late Celal, my loyal garden help who died of a heart attack last year. This little baby has also been named Celal. Yup, Old Celal, and New Celal. I sat by the baby's head and began rocking the cradle with her while we chatted.

Suddenly, the dogs began barking. Dudu and I looked up. A white haired man appeared at the entrance to Dudu's land. I recognised him immediately as the man who owns the land with the Wisdom Carob. I hadn't seen him since mid-summer when he'd harvested the pods.

"Do you reckon we can get our tractor up this road?" he called from the track, while shooing off Dudu's polka dot mongrel which was yapping at his ankles.

"Yeees," said Dudu. "If the pomegranate truck made it, you can." Then she turned to me. She was sitting at baby Celal's feet. I was at his crown. "They've cut a carob back there. It was sick," she said rocking the infant so vigorously his head shook.

I sat stock still and felt my eyeballs straining. No, no, no.

"He's cut down that amazing carob tree? That beautiful, massive old one?"

Dudu grinned at me affectionately. She found my emotional attachment to trees somewhat unfathomable.

"Not all of it," she cawed through her wrinkles. "Just the dead boughs. The tree's still alive."

I left Dudu's in haste. Rotty the dog and I marched down the earthen track (well I marched, Rotty skipped and jumped and ran in and out of the forest oblivious of my concern). We passed my land, and walked along the forest edge. The dirt avenue opened onto the Wisdom Carob land. Mount Olympos rose in the distance, his southern flank bathed in coppery fire. I stopped. The umbrella of Wisdom Carob was gone. In fact most of her was gone. There were a couple of branches left with plumes of green spurting out.

I expected to feel devastated, but I didn't. Even from this distance, I knew it was all alright. But I decided to wait until the next day, until the owner had cleared the wood from the site, before inspecting any closer.

It was yesterday that I approached the small fountain of green that is the New Wisdom Carob. What I saw made my arms prickle. The owner had cut off exactly the same two boughs I'd been sitting on two days prior. It was too eerie for words. The muscles along my spine shivered as I took it in. When I inspected the severed limbs, they gaped like ligneous arteries, hollow and dead. Dead boughs drain the life of a tree. They slow its growth. If they are diseased, they can even kill it. Then something else dawned on me. I noted with intrigue that the severed boughs had been the original trunks of the tree. What was left were two new trunks that had sprouted from the old. There was nothing remaining of the original carob. Yet it was still very much alive. Just disconcertingly New.

Hmm. Yes. And isn't that the way of it? For all of us? All the time?

I turned from the tree. As I ambled along the forest edge back home, I considered the various versions of me scattered along the tracks of my past, the dead limbs of my youth, the severed branches, the hollowed out pieces of me I'd forgotten about. Some of them no doubt infecting me. Those Old selves felt like strangers. *Was I really once* her? I wondered. And yet somehow, those defunct Kerrys begot this one. And this one will beget the New. And once it does, it too will be the Old.

Perhaps it already is.

I arrived home. That evening something else dawned on me. I searched for my wallet (which only sees the light of day about once a week). Soon enough I found what I was looking for. A slip of paper from my dentist given to me two weeks earlier. There on the white square I read the date and time; 11 am, 18 November 2015, extraction. Two of my wisdom teeth are slowly rotting. If I leave them in they'll slowly infect the gum. It's time to let them go. Wisdom teeth. Wisdom trees. Wisdom only knows what's coming next. But something is. And it's new.

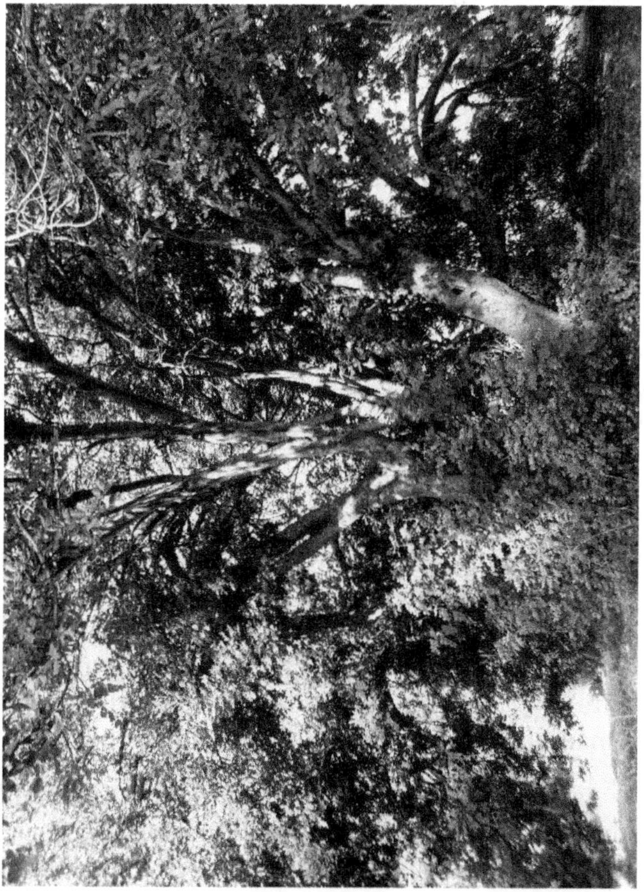

Non-Participation

December 2015

Dedicated to a seven-year-old boy called Maxim.

Perhaps it's simply my circle, but these days, all about me I see disgust for The System. The way the world is set up. The way the majority of the world's people are used as toilet paper for the minority that can pay for it. The wars in Africa and the Middle East which boost a number of G7 economies via arms sales. The environmental havoc being wreaked so that CEOs can watch numbers on a bank balance rise. The media tripe specifically designed to pit one group against another. The amount of people who seem to swallow that tripe.

Strange. Over here in Mudland, that System seems no more than a bad dream I slip into whenever I venture online. Right now, the December sunlight is gracing the tips of the trees. I'm watching the pines rise in feathery clusters. A metre from my window, a star agama has thrown his blue head back to grab a ray of extra UV. Dragonflies and butterflies flit over the remaining marigolds. It's another dimension.

As I absorb the clear breath of nature, I remember something. Someone. A small Taiwanese boy called Maxim. I think about him whenever I consider The System.

I was a teacher for about 15 years and it taught me a bit about controlling groups of people. A traditional classroom is a type of mini-state; a nation of 30 small(ish) beings and a non-elected adult manager wrestling with a largely meaningless curriculum in a concrete box that wouldn't normally be deemed large enough for a couple to cohabit. It's actually a microcosm of the greater System it is part of.

Over the years of classroom teaching one thing always baffled me; the students never revolted. There were 30 of them and one of me after all. Sometimes they were teenagers and towered over me. It should have been anarchy. It never was. You see, teachers learn something airily termed 'classroom management'. It used to be called 'discipline' or 'classroom control', which was at the very least more honest. And I'm ashamed to say, it was something I was good at.

Yes, I'm a recovering autocrat.

Any trained teacher knows, one of the most effective ways to 'manage' students is to divide them into teams and make them compete for a paltry prize. Yup, Machiavelli lives on, even in 21st century education. I can attest that the strategy works brilliantly. You experience very little dissidence, and it's cheap. In Taiwan, a few stickers or a packet of pencils was all it took for students to do almost anything. In the UK boys school I worked in, it was a fantasy football league. It's basically party politics in a classroom. Divide and rule, it never fails.

Another convenient method for 'directing' 30 free-willed souls is to offer them limited choices. You never ask; 'What would you like to do today?' Instead, you put forward two or three choices. The students are so busy debating the optimum choice, they forget all other options. Like rats in an alley, they are forced along the paths the teacher assigns.

I was taught both these strategies (and plenty more) on a PGCE, and it was at a very progressive university in London.

As it goes with schools, so it goes with populations. Give the poor saps a vote, offer them three ropey candidates, keep them busy squabbling over it, throw them a few meaningless rewards if they slog their guts out their entire life, meanwhile...

My last experience with classroom teaching was in a primary school in Taiwan. It was the end of my career. I hated The System I was now once again a part of, and did my utmost to controvert it. I began to experiment. Instead of managing, I had a bash at liberating.

Initially, when I discussed my ideas with my students, I was surprised none of them wanted to hear they weren't free. Sometimes, out of sheer frustration, I began to ask older classes, 'Do you think this school is a democracy?' Most were adamant that it was, even when I pointed out that they had no say in what they did for the entire day, no say in who taught them, no say in the classroom management rules, and no say in whether to attend the class or not. They were *legally* bound to be there. Of the few that did consider the implications of this, most looked as though the foundations of their universe had dissolved. When the truth is unpleasant, folk generally opt for denial.

And yet, happily there's always an exception, isn't there? You can always find one or two little gems in a class who see through the ruse. Back in Taiwan, one of these was a Grade 2 boy called Maxim. Maxim was small for his age, quiet but not shy, and he loved animals, especially pigs. He would resolutely sketch animals all over his Maths book, his Science book and his English book. He thought the rewards were stupid, and didn't participate in the class unless it was about animals. If you made him stay in at break, he didn't care, because he would just draw more animals. One day, I was standing at the blackboard chalking up team points, and I finally realised there was nothing I could do about it.

Children who can't or won't fit into the education system have always been labelled something. These days it's ADHD, before it was 'difficult' or 'a sod'. Whatever the label, these are the system challengers, and there are two kinds; there are the protesters who disrupt the class using any range of methods from shouting to violence. Then there are the non-participaters like Maxim who aren't rude or destructive, but simply don't join in.

Protesters and non-participators.

As time went by in Taiwan, I noticed something about the protester students that gave me reason to pause. They unwittingly upheld the system. They were always a tiny minority, a fringe group the mainstream didn't aspire to being, and as such were a deterrent for the rest of the students. Certainly, if the entire class had risen up and begun throwing chairs about, or run round the room screaming, there wouldn't be much a teacher could do about it. But that never happens. Because a protester is in herself a negation, she is not really offering a creative alternative to The System, just a reaction to it. The predominant energy that the protester taps into is anger.

Non-participators, however, are a different kettle of fish. For an autocrat, they are notoriously difficult to deal with. What do you do when someone simply doesn't join in? Even if you resort to the most draconian measures available, they will at best be half-participating. It's as if they are sucking the juice out of the engine of the system drop by invisible drop.

Maxim wasn't angry, aggressive or openly challenging. He was polite and a rather cute little boy. Because he wasn't disruptive, and because even the most dogged leaders have limited energy, it was easier to let Maxim sketch animals than try to coerce him into joining the class. Without realising it, I soon found myself incorporating more lessons on the subject of animals just for his benefit. It also dawned on me that after a term of Maxim never completing his workbook and drawing animals everywhere, that it really didn't make much difference to anything. The workbook was on the curriculum, but it was by and large nonsense. Maxim could still read and add up. Hmm.

In the end, I decided to get rid of the workbook for the others too. I chose the most useful pages for the students to work through, and let them quickly copy the answers for the rest (I was also being checked on by superiors and would be hauled up in front of a supervisor if pages of the workbook were missing). Eventually, I went the whole hog. I let my Grade 2 class do whatever they felt like. Was there anarchy? Was there war? Were there 30 seven-year-olds running wild around the class because they were bored? Did the world collapse? Did they all become stupid, uneducated fools? Nope. None of the above.

The projects those pupils came up with once the curriculum was abandoned took my breath away. Some designed huge crossword puzzles for their friends, others created storybooks and hung them around the class for the others to read, some made model rockets, others read books. One boy just sat and daydreamed. Maxim drew picture after picture of animals. And when he was done with contemporary ones, he drew dinosaurs. Brilliantly. Expertly.

Take note: Thirty students. One of them changed the system, just by not participating and doing what he loved. This is big news for those of us who realise the majority don't or won't see through the ruse. Ever.

Now, I have been of an activist temperament most of my life; opinionated, rebellious and passionate about justice and the environment. I have a big mouth and don't mind using it. I've taken part in protests. I have voted in every election I was eligible for, both in the UK and Turkey. Even when there has been no candidate worth a minute of my time, I've still voted. I've participated.

And that's just what The System loves; people who participate.

After Taiwan, I took a leaf out of Maxim's pig-decorated practice book. I donned a pair of wellies, left the world of work and began scribbling notes on the internet. Why? Because I like writing. I also like building. I *love* not doing a day job. I live on about £200 a month, so my contribution to those CEOs' bank accounts is pretty minimal. I'm not plugged into a grid.

Of course, I'm not System free. I use the internet and pay a company to provide it. Maxim wasn't System free either. He was still at school after all. And like Maxim, I do my best to only participate in what I love, and pull my energy out of that which I don't. Every detail counts. Every moment I'm voting with my soul.

Because in truth, The System isn't some vague malign entity 'out there'. We are a part of it. We create it. And with every single action we take, no matter how small it may look, we are changing it.

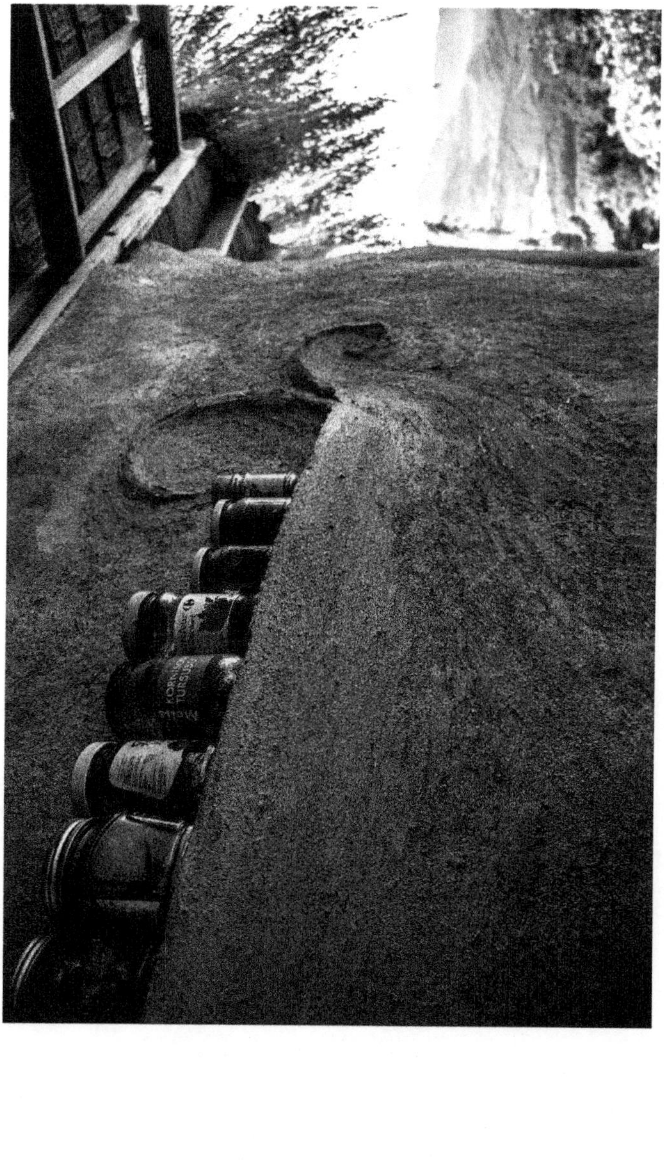

2016

Workmen and Hell

January 2016

There is a special corner of hell reserved for tradespeople, and it's littered with broken promises and half-finished porches. The flooring (I'm thinking the Devil likes parquet) is paint-spattered, the tools are all over the garden, and the thermostat is *still* broken. But don't worry. The heating will be turned down next week. Promise. On my life. Seriously, you can *trust* me. Next week. It'll be done.

Nowadays it's a rare day that I hire help. Over the past four years (*Four*? Four have they gone. Where?) I've developed triceps and quadriceps, and many other muscles sounding oddly like dinosaurs that I'd never heard of. More importantly, I've learned the techniques. And yes there's always a technique for everything, be it rock dragging or machete swinging. There's even a technique (which Celal showed me – oh Celal you are missed) for hacking out monster thorn bushes involving a rake and a well-applied wellie, but that's a whole other chapter.

This year I called upon a labourer twice. Once in spring to cut the grass, and once in autumn to chop my wood. Both occasions drove me nuts. It was akin to dragging a belligerent donkey up a steep bramble-throttled hill. So three months ago, when a certain someone, who out of loyalty and fondness shall not be named, explained he had a few weeks free while the courgettes in his greenhouse grew, I leapt on the possibility.

"Yes, I'll take care of that wood for you, no hassle," he said.

Three months ago. October came and went. November arrived. My wood shed still gaped hungrily. Eventually, I decided action was necessary, so when I saw the aforementioned personage driving to his greenhouse one morning, I blocked his path.

"Hey, I need that wood cutting. Today! Seriously. Rain is coming and I'm woodless," I yelled.

A tousled head poked out of the driver's window and the mouth within it yawned. "Hmm, we're tying the courgettes today."

I widened my eyes. "But you told me you had time. Like a *month* ago."

The aforementioned personage revved his engine. I folded my arms and remained put in the centre of the road.

"Alright. But I can't do four hours today. Just two."

"Two's fine. I'll take two hours. Just cut me some wood."

So the aforementioned personage came and chopped half the wood. *Better than nothing*, I thought. Winter settled. I threw log after log into the wood burner, and soon enough the wood stack was once more depleted. "Here we go again", I groaned.

Thus a month ago, I took a long, deep breath and attempted to wring another two hours of wood cutting from the dishcloth of labourer time. I called at the aforementioned personage's house. He said he'd turn up the next day. He didn't. I called him that evening, and the next evening. Every time he said he'd be there either today or tomorrow. Two more weeks passed, and I was down to about five logs. The trouble was, because he had cut half the wood already, only a two-hour cutting stint remained. No one else was going to trek over to my land for two hours work. I was over a barrel.

And this is it, isn't it? They grab you by the short and curlies and then you're stuck. Your foundations are in, but the builder hasn't shown up for a month since. You paid for the pine six months ago, but the carpenter spent the cash on Rakı. Half your wood is cut and now burned. The other half is waiting, and the weather forecast is showing minus 5 degrees centigrade for the coming week. The sense of powerless in the face of this task incompletion is phenomenal. You need the workman. He doesn't show up. It's *desperate*. I felt a wrecking ball of anger begin swinging inside me; a plutonium pendulum of mass destruction. "Fine. Just fine," I muttered to no one in particular.

The next morning I wandered over to the aforementioned personage's greenhouse. I gabbled at him non-stop until he pleaded for me to leave. I did the same again in the afternoon.

"Alright, alright; I'll come at four today. I promise," he said as he tinkered with something under the bonnet of his car.

"If you're not coming, you'd better call me," I said. *Or what, Kerry? Honestly, what are you going to do?*

I returned home. It was two in the afternoon. I waited. I tried to be patient. I tried not to think the worst or to feel desperate.

Time passed, as it does. Four o'clock came and went. The pendulum inside me began swinging. Quarter past four. Half past four arrived. Snatching my phone from the table, I called Dudu. "Have you seen him?" I yelled into the phone.

"Oh, yes. He left five minutes ago," she replied cheerily. Then added, "Drove clean off he did." Just to stoke the fire a little.

Boom! The wrecking ball smashed through my frontal lobes, destroyed all synapses related to politeness and reason, it took out every gate of self-control and crushed any self-conscious care. I was well and truly pissed off, as we say in the United Kingdom.

I stormed to the shed, yanked out the chainsaw and roared some words which would even have caused the workmen in their corner of hell to blink. An image of me charging up to the greenhouse with the chainsaw, and driving its steel fangs into each and every courgette plant, bloomed happily inside me. Courgette soup for breakfast, dinner and tea for you lot, I cackled. The fantasy ended with me sawing a 'K' Zorro-style into the polytunnel plastic, and stalking off.

Back in reality, I exhaled, then walked away from the shed, chainsaw in hand.

Now, you shouldn't start a chainsaw when you're fuming. It's really not a good idea.

Except when it is.

Anger gets a bad name, but it's like money, a knife, or indeed a chainsaw. It all depends how you use it. If you refrain from fixating on the object of your anger, and tap into the power beneath, it's amazing stuff. As long as you don't actually transform someone's greenhouse of courgettes into a massive vegan smoothie, all is well. It's all about putting the energy to good use. And let's face it, I had a use for it. It was loitering at the edge of my land in huge, bark-encased stumps.

Instead of heading for the polytunnels, I made for those wheels of pine the aforementioned personage was supposed to cut. I'd never cut a trunk that large before, and I wasn't sure I'd be able to push through it. I started my death beast up. She roared pleasingly. Rage turned to power, and it surged through my body like a mass-produced eighties rock song. The blade churned through the wood. One huge hunk fell away. Then another. On and on.

An hour later, I couldn't believe my eyes, but I had most of the set cut into slices. The light was failing. I didn't care. I was so pumped, I yanked out the axe and began hacking right there and then. There is no job better for a bad mood than wood splitting. With every slew the world became better and brighter.

As darkness fell, I charged up and down the land with the wheelbarrow ferrying the cut wood into the shed. And it felt so *good*. I did it. It cost me nothing. I burned fat, built more muscles with weird names, and expelled vats of negative energy. The wood was ready. I was saved. It's quite marvellous when you look at it. I had no idea the point of the hired hand was to drive you to such a state of fury you managed the task yourself.

And *this* is the beauty of home building. *This* is why you move off-grid and become independent. *This* is the unparalleled freedom you are granted when you learn a few skills and get in shape. You never need suffer that tradesman torment again. Ever. You are empowered. They can go to their corner in hell (if indeed they can get in, because no doubt the door handle is loose and comes off in their hands), while you sit back, light the fire, and admire your handiwork.

Sigh (long and contented).

So now it seems I only need a workman *once* a year.

Hmm. Four months until spring and the grass cutting. Oh dear, I'm feeling anxious already.

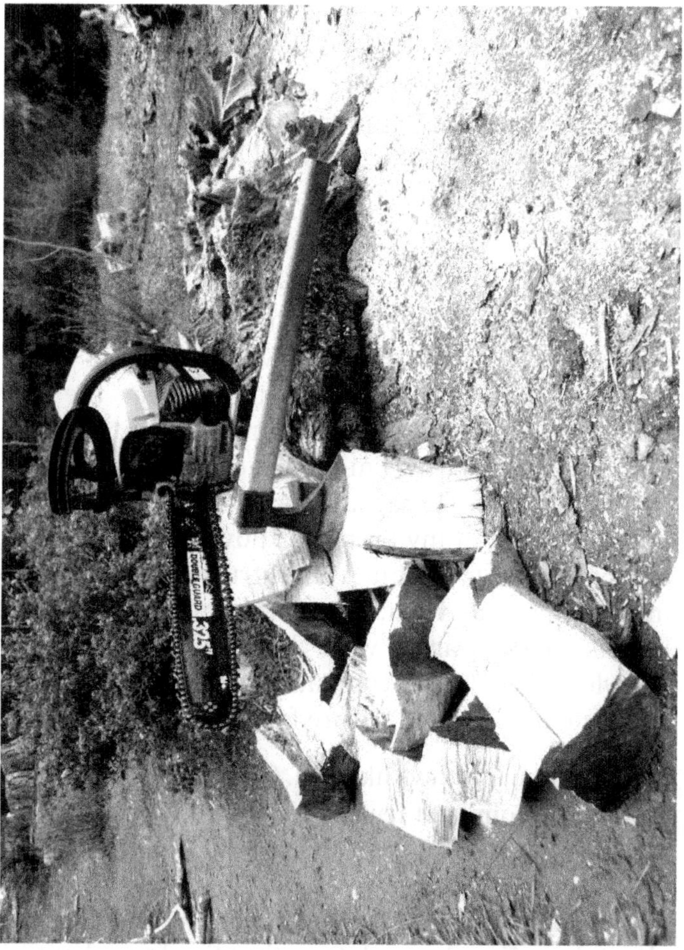
DOUBLE GUARD
.325"

The Lizards Dance

February 2016

"Lizards are just walking right up to us, locusts are hanging out with me having a shower, it's very strange. The robin...he sings to me while I pee." said a friend of mine who's looking after my mud home, while I make a short trip to the UK.

Ah how I smiled when I listened to his voice message. Yes, the robin is a cheeky little devil. I know him well. All of a sudden my mind sailed out of my dad's living room in Essex. I was back there in my Eden, with the butterflies fluttering over the kale plants, and the squirrels scampering along the pines. You see, *this* is why I'm rather cagey about people entering the land. Because it's true. The wildlife within the magic ring of my property knows me. The beasts, birds and insects trust me. And I trust them. In fact, as my friend pointed out, there are now generations of insects and lizards with handed down genetic knowledge that 'The Human' loves them. We are a connected ecosystem. We are family.

But I wasn't always like this. Once upon a time, I too killed scorpions and feared the boar. Ten years ago, I would have laid poison and traps, thinking it was simply the way things were, and that I had to protect myself to survive. I wasn't even particularly bothered about dogs. I've changed. Or rather I've *been* changed, and nature is the transformer.

Nature comes laden with gifts so extraordinary, we moderns don't even believe them possible. When you approach it as a friend or kin, you will witness miracles, some of which leave you slack-jawed. Let's take the army of ants nesting just outside my kitchen. Ten years ago, I'd have been sure I had to get rid of them. But now? Well, I have observed these incredible insects. At some mysterious agreed-upon day and time, they congregate on the kitchen floor. Masses of them. The earth turns into a dark moving carpet. I wait. An hour later when they have moved on, I see. The ants have cleaned the floor. Perfectly. Yet they never delve into my honey, nor my carob molasses which sit in open jars upon the shelf. How? Why? It is indeed strange.

Typically, when we hear survival 'into the wild' type stories, machismo is the name of the game. This is tragic. Of course, machismo has nothing to do with masculinity. It is an aberration; a fake set of values – generally violent and emotion crushing – parading as bravery and hiding cowardice. The glorified wilderness survival tales we have thrown at us in film or book form are a neatly packaged slice of this machismo. They are sold to a modern world that has become so tedious in its convenience that the only excitement left is bungee jumping, cocaine or having an affair. Thus the wild is peddled as the ultimate dangerous adventure. The last frontier.

Yet nature isn't a frontier. It's where we all came from. It's home! Even the word 'survival' when talking about living in the wild seems inappropriate, because it is based on a fiction that nature is some sort of alien monster out to attack us, rather than the very thing that sustains us. The natural world is where we belong, the place we are *designed* for. Anyone who has spent a significant time alone in nature and attempted to get to know it a little, realises this. The indigenous peoples of the forests, those who have evaded the great train of 'civilisations' realise this. You don't see them indiscriminately bludgeoning any animal that crosses their path. They clutch the last remaining shreds of ancient wisdom in their cultures, namely that everything has its place.

Nature is alive, and like all living beings, she's responsive. She is also very fair; not sentimental, but fair. What you give is what you get with nature. I've seen it over and over again. You enter a territory and become the savage hunter, then you will at some point become the hunted. You will not be trusted. You will have set up an energy field of fear and aggression, and every living being that enters that field will reflect that back to you. Hence why I don't own a gun, nor do I allow them on my property. I don't want that energy circulating on my land.

The reason I can live in The Mud alone and feel safe, is because I *am* safe. The energy of my land is one of love and respect, not fear. There is no struggle to survive. In fact, as time goes on the land provides more and more in the most incredible ways. There is a delicious wild plant known locally as turnip grass. It's rich in iron and vitamin C, and very versatile to cook with. Last year I spoke to the land and expressed how much I love that plant. This year it has sprouted all over the lower end of my garden. I've such a surplus, I now give it to Dudu. Struggle? Survival? Nature feels a lot more like Santa Claus to me.

The wildlife has taught me one final lesson; we humans have been blessed with the power to create the emotional signature of our territories. We can choose the energy we want to emit, and the attitudes we hold. Me? I want paradise on Earth. I want a world full of love, respect and kindness. I want wonder and magic. Utopian dream? Not for me. Well, definitely not within *my* space. Because this land, The Mud, *is* my world, and within those boundaries my rules apply.

We may not be able to change other people, or dictate what they do with their spaces. That's just as well. Who knows what's right in the larger picture anyway? Still, it takes conviction and effort to maintain a positive state of mind. I struggle when I hear hunters killing tiny birds, apparently just for the fun of it. And I'm no innocent. Things *have* been killed inadvertently here, and once from a lack of self-belief. Yes, at times I've wanted to buy a rifle and shoot back at hunters too. But I've not given up. Like my freshly germinated spinach seeds, I just keep pushing upwards, striving bit by bit for the light, trying to hold the kind of world I want within me. And now I see. My space has responded. It has been created. The gunmen have moved away. The land holds the vibration. Geckos clean my saucepans. Swallow ballets are performed over my gazebo. Wild boar career through my land, yet leave my potatoes untouched. And now the lizards dance and the robin sings, not just for me, but for my friends.

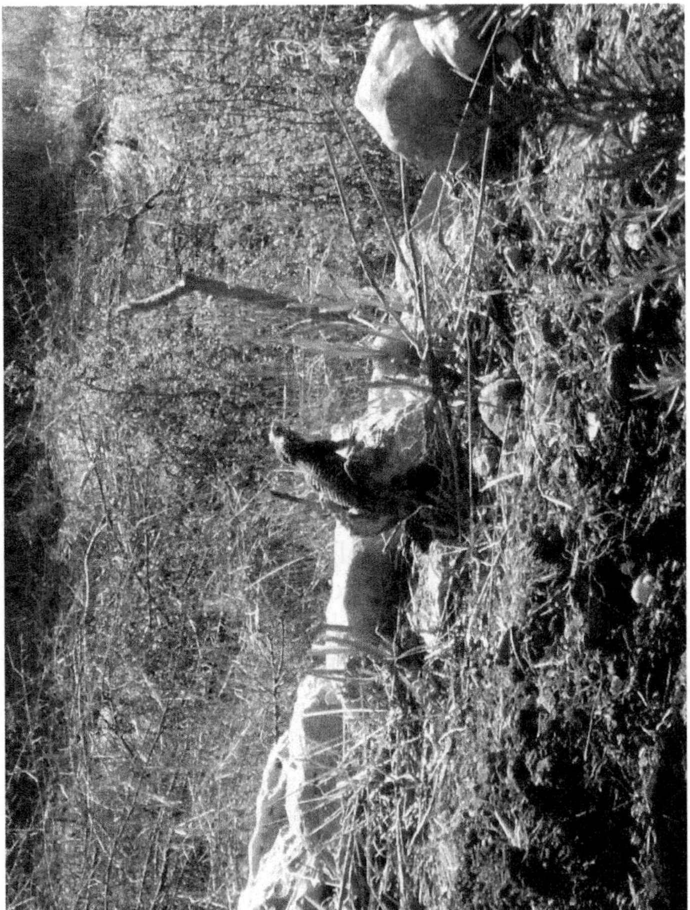

Where am I Going?

March 2016

The sky is a little standoffish this cool March morning. A field of ploughed cumulus. Neither up nor down. Sort of in between. As if it can't quite make its mind up whether its cloudy furrows will bring forth sunshine or rain.

The apricot tree, however, has had enough of fence-sitting. The pink buds she's been holding onto so tightly slipped through her fingers today. The first blossom of the year is now out. And this is nature. This is life. Cycle upon cycle. One phase begets another, and another, and another. And each year, although spring inevitably follows winter and winter follows autumn, the garden climbs higher. The trees stretch taller.

But what's this got to do with The Mud Series, and my writing? Well, because everything evolves in seasonal phases, including The Mud and myself. *Mud Ball* hasn't yet been out a year, and happily many have been asking about the sequel. Naturally, I'm writing. I'm always writing. I love the feel of words carving pictures on the screen, and the memories they attempt to preserve.

There are three specific phases (or seasons) to my Mud adventure: Transformation (winter), Empowerment (spring) and Independence (summer). *Mud Ball* is the second part of that trilogy. It describes the spring of this adventure, the visible burgeoning of a new home. The very speed at which my house appeared had a spring-like magic about it. One minute there was nothing, the next an earthbag house. Building my own home granted me many gifts, but one of the most striking was an unshakeable sense of personal power.

However, there was a winter before that spring. When I first moved onto this land, I was depressed and lost. The garden of my life seemed to have shed every leaf. As I've stated many times, this off-grid lark was never a dream of mine. I was thrown into it. Yet that psychological winter was perhaps the most magical time here. I still hanker after those wild woman moments, and fantasize about reliving my 'lost in the woods' soul journey. You see, it was because of the powers I learned over those houseless months – commonly disbelieved magical powers and forgotten ancient skills – that I've lived happily alone up here for five years. This piece of land changed me into someone completely new. Moving off-grid and into nature *will* change you. It will blow apart everything you thought you knew about yourself. And just like a seed on the verge of germination, you either let go of the husk of your old form, and transform into a plant, or you die.

So the story I'm two thirds of the way through now is a prequel. *Dirt Witch* delves into those six months under canvas, before the earthbag adventure began. I was terrified of boar, more terrified of snakes, and the first few weeks were spent cowering inside my tent after dark. I didn't know how to use a spade, nor did I have the faintest idea how to grow a plant. Connecting with ants, scorpions and geckos wasn't even in my galaxy of experience.

After *Dirt Witch* and *Mud Ball*, there is of course the conclusion to the tale. Those who read Mud Ball will know, at the end of the earthbag adventure, I had to return to Taiwan and teach. Those six months focussed me. After that, I aimed to become independent of the system, survive without money. Did I manage that? And to what extent? What does it really mean to be independent, after all? Can we ever be? These are the questions I wrangle and wrestle with in the final part of The Mud Series, just as I did in my life.

So there you have it: the winter, spring and summer on The Mud. But there are four seasons, aren't there? What about autumn?

Autumn has snuck up on me. I can feel it, despite the lust-driven strides of the tortoises and the pollen dusting my solar panels. I knew something was coming the moment The Wisdom Carob spoke to me this November. There's no stasis in nature. The seasons roll on. And life always wants us to grow taller, stretch higher, so that our canopies might touch virgin parts of the sky. Sometimes it breaks off entire branches...

So knowing what is inevitably before me, I'm beginning to hoard my mud treasures. I scamper through each day collecting kernels of beauty, wisdom and magic, stuffing them into the pockets of my memory. As the clouds moil and raindrops fall, I inhale each moment. My harvest has been bounteous. My store cupboards are full. I'm ready.

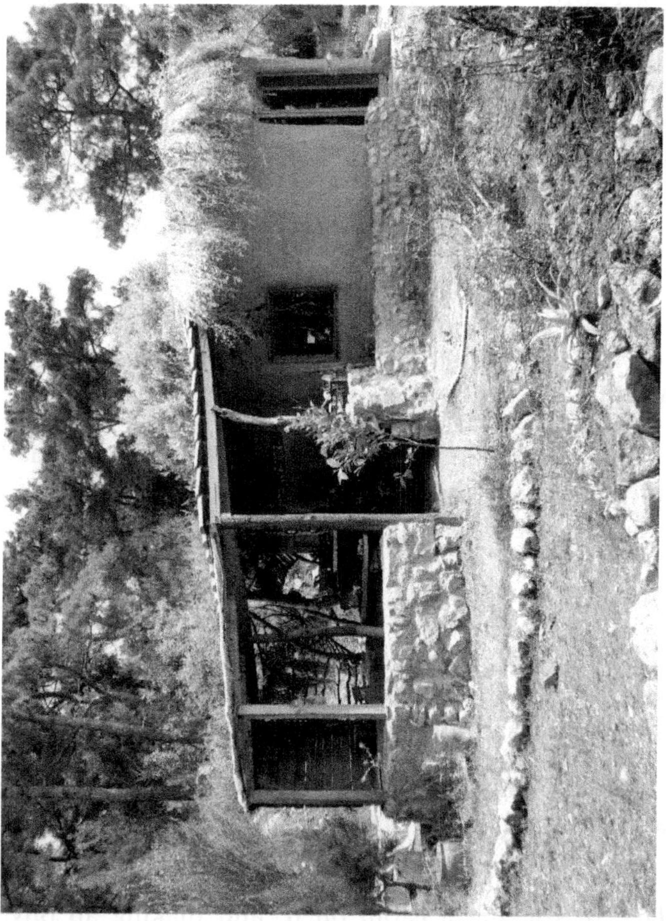

Bulldozers

April 2016

I was wakened by a screech so violent, I thought the earth had split in two. As I dragged my fingers across my bleary eyes, I realised it wasn't an explosion, but the crashing of a massive rock. The ground was shuddering. The house was vibrating. Fear filed out of its network of submerged tunnels and formed a solid army of dread.

There was another crash, and a terrible crack. Beyond that I could hear the gruff roar of an engine. And I knew in that instant it was over.

In fact, I'd known this was coming. Dudu had informed me of the plan a couple of weeks earlier. But I hadn't expected it to be like this.

"Oof the pomegranates are such a pain. Need too much water, they do, and we don't have enough rain," Dudu had said when I popped round for some lemons one day. "So they've decided to split the land up into three." She was talking about her children.

"And...?" I had moved my stool a little closer to her, wondering what was in store.

"My daughter's gonna take the part by your land. They're sticking a cabin on it, and making an olive grove. Digger's coming in a couple of weeks to clear it."

I'd heaved a sigh of relief that day. Because since I've been here, there has been talk of a road being carved between me and Dudu. This new plan would put pay to the road forever. And an olive grove is about as good as it gets. Olives can be grown organically, need little water and create beautiful evergreen orchards. Even the building concept possessed angles of optimism. A small log cabin perched on the far corner of the land.

Yet two weeks later, I was standing at the fence between mine and Dudu's land, tears rolling down my cheeks, knowing it was over.

Whenever I hear the grinding tread of an excavator, or the teeth-jarring scrape of its bucket on rock, my skin turns to glass. Because mass destruction is occurring. Habitats are being wrecked. Ecosystems are being wiped out. In seconds, ancient trees are ripped asunder (and unless you are dead yourself, you hear the life torn viscerally out of them). It doesn't sound much different to a bomb going off in a shopping mall. And if you're a hedgehog, or a snail, or a sleeping dormouse, no doubt it isn't any different at all.

Not that I'm in any position to preach a sermon. I *also* had my land bulldozed ten years ago, before I changed. Before the land changed me. I'm not even completely against dozers. Like everything, if they are used sparingly and thoughtfully, they can be excellent tools, for digging a pool say, or creating a flat space for a house. It's the loveless, uninspired, destroy-everything-within-the-fence-without-even-getting-to-know-what's-there approach that sends my hair darting out on end.

It took three days for the excavator to complete its dirty deed next door. In truth, as land mauls go, this was gentle. They left the majority of the mature trees standing; the olives, almond trees and a carob. But as that mechanical claw beat the branches from pines and turned the land inside out, it sank in. This was no longer my private world. No longer my secret garden. Someone was moving in next door. I realised the Wisdom Carob had spoken a premonitory truth back in November. It was time to let go. I could feel the hand of life on my shoulder, gently pushing me on.

This year was the turning point for my valley. Since February a grand total of four plots have been bulldozed in my area alone. None of them are visible, but all of them are within a kilometre of my land. People are coming. It's getting busier. Though this may not necessarily be the bleak cliché it appears. We're not talking multistorey concrete monstrosities. Dudu's children, for example, are building with a dream in their hearts. To escape the city. To grow their own food. To live more peacefully. This may be the feathery tip of a new wing beating out a more minimalist path across Turkey's socio-cultural sky. And I'm all for it.

But on a personal level the dozers woke me up. I love, nay *need*, my privacy. There are times when I don't want to see a human face for a week or more. I yearn to lose myself in the forest and hear her quiet message. Hear her twitterings, her scamperings, the whisper of her trees. And through them hear myself.

I grieved for three days after the bulldozing. I wondered if I'd get used to the change, whether I should accept it and adapt to it. Perhaps in time I'd warm to it? One day may be I'd be grateful for the company? Eventually, however, my mind, forced as it was out of its comfort zone, dared to face the alternative.

Not once in the five years I've been here have I ever considered letting this space go. I have imagined growing old here. Dying here. This land and I have grown together after all. It's both my child and my mother. But when I finally allowed myself to wander the alien territory beyond my home, my eyes opened wide. Wading across the boundary of my rigid future plans and possessive clingings, I stepped into a field of possibility. And as I roamed a little more extensively within it, I realised it wasn't just a field, but a vast and rambling continent, a wilderness of new adventures waiting to be explored.

The longer I spent in my imagined terra incognita, the more alive I felt. Ideas sprang forth. Visions burst into being. And soon, I realised, new life was flowing. In my veins. In my land's veins. And in the veins of the world.

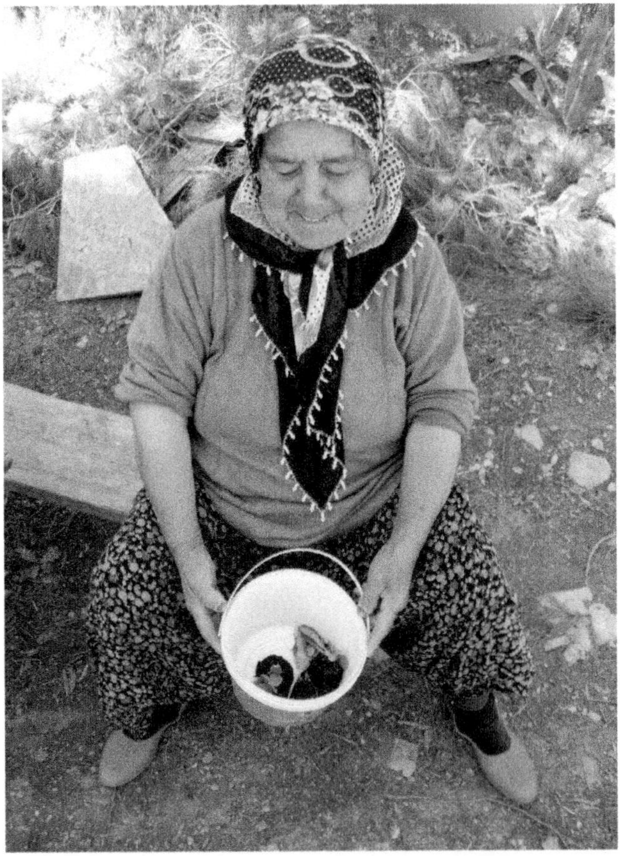

What is a Home?

June 2016

How precious a home is. How personal. Idiosyncratic. Like a fingerprint, no home is ever the same as the next. Despite the mass-produced efforts of DIY Homebases, our homes remain unique, even if our houses are not. Because a home is so much more than a brick and mortar case. So much deeper. So much wider. It's a world. A series of concentric circles, expanding ever outward. But from what?

Running my finger over the grainy walls, I attempt to draw it all back into me. This creation. The inset beads, the painted stones, each individual window frame. For I've been living inside a sculpture. Many times I wasn't sure as it morphed and grew, whether it was in fact my product, or possessed a life and will of its own.

Yet despite illusions a home, no matter how delicately and intimately arranged, is not us. I learn this now, and it is a rude awakening. As I slowly unpick the loops and peel them back from my soul, my eyes water. For it smarts, this letting go.

With each passing day another ring drops to the ground. And another. Until one day soon I'll stand bare, shorn of possessions, stripped of my façades.

Just a self. A well of being. Naked. Free. Ready to create once more.

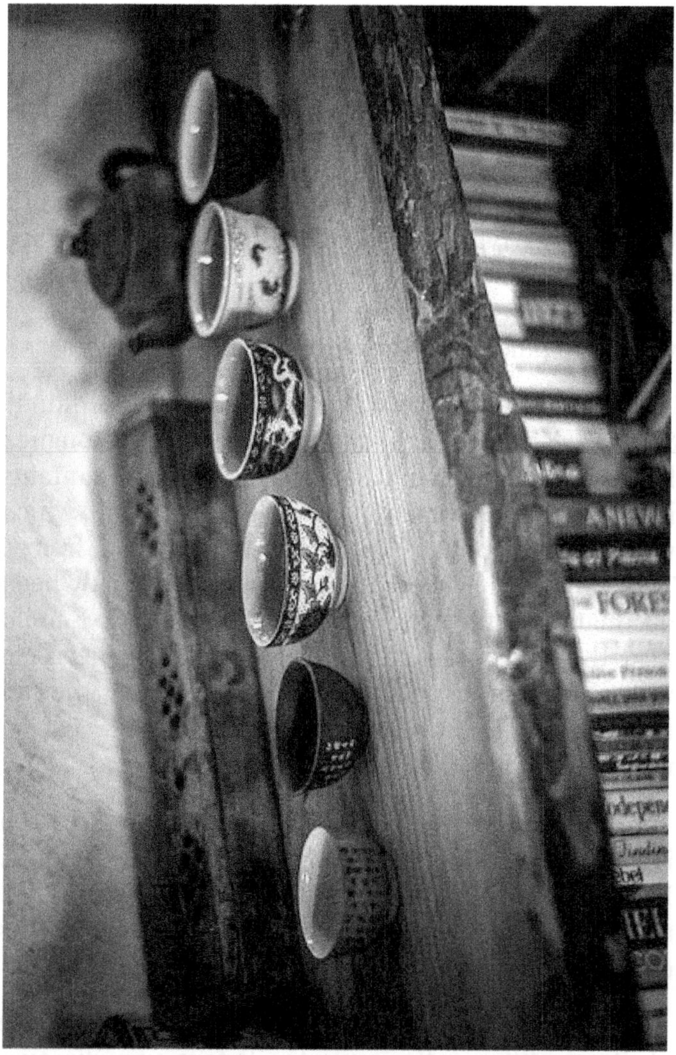

Fire Fire!

July 2016

"Erm. I feel I ought to let you know. A second fire has started in the valley and it's moving in your direction. Very fast."

I held the phone to my ear. As with every morning, I was sitting typing into my computer. A thick drape was fixed over the front window; a fabric aegis against a molten barrage of sun. Did I hold my breath as I walked to pluck back the curtain? I don't remember.

Now, I knew there was a forest fire. Who didn't? Since the 24th June, an insatiable orange-tongued hydra has been hissing and spitting in the mountains behind my mud home. It is goaded by the wind, which whips those tongues into a tree-devouring frenzy. Thousands of hectares of forestland had already been decimated by the time I took the phone call. I could hear the helicopters slicing across the valley ferrying water over the brow. But until that moment, the fire had limited its rampage to the other side of the mountain range. Our valley had been protected.

I yanked the curtain from its hook. The breath inside me seemed to stick to the walls of my epiglottis. Because there, just over a small ridge, what looked like about five kilometres from my home, smoke was churning into the air.

Let it be known, it is unwise to consume a cafetière of strong filter coffee minutes before you discover you're bang on the path of a forest fire. There were a number of sharp spasms in my chest, and I started whirring round and round my mud circle like a trapped wasp. I drank water. I breathed slowly and cursed the caffeine. Because I needed to focus. Get calm. Get straight.

This isn't my first forest fire. I've seen a few. But not driving full throttle in the direction of my home. Five kilometres is nothing in forest fire terms. If the wind continued on its incendiary path, I guessed I had half an hour to save myself, my sick dog who couldn't walk, and... and...? To add spice to the challenge, I don't own a car. Only a motorbike. My belly lurched when I remembered that. Shaking, I picked up my phone and called Dudu, who is as automobileless as I am. She was unflappable.

"Oh yes, I can see it. The kids are here so don't you worry," she said.

Ramazan who owned the greenhouses below me was less stoic. "We have five minutes. *Five* minutes! And it will be here." His voice broke down. Because the fire signified the end of livelihoods, the end of homes, and the end of lives as well.

Places like Turkey (you know, Muslim, Middle Eastern places) get a nasty rap in the Western media. And that media is ignorant. One beautiful thing about this land that Westerners from afar might not grasp, is that you are never truly alone here, no matter how odd or misshapen you might be. I could have pretty much dialled any number randomly, and as long as I omitted the Istanbul code, someone would have come to save me, or sent someone else to do the same. Within minutes I had two offers of escape. While I waited for one of them to arrive, I began packing. For the most part it was easy. Though later that evening when I unpacked my rucksack again, I did ponder on what exactly I planned to do with my sander. Especially as I only remembered the head.

The reason I could squash my life in a bag in less than fifteen minutes, was due to priorities. Nothing mattered much except my dog. Everything could go up in smoke. My home could become the world's largest cob oven. My kitchen could disappear. It would all be OK. I've lost and left homes before. They can be rebuilt. But my dog had to survive. I love her desperately. Everyone around me knows it.

Now, I'm not partial to these "there are two kinds of people" statements. But sorry, there really are two separate clans regarding dogs; those that love them and those that can't see what the other group are so obsessed about. Until three years ago, I was part of the second group. I was a nature lover, but never understood how anyone could become so attached to a four-legged fur ball that couldn't even speak, never mind discuss the meaning of life or appreciate an art gallery. I was one of those who found this pet-nurturing lark rather a lot of over-sentimental tripe. I was also one of those who would exclaim outraged, "People care more about their dogs than they do their fellow *humans*!" And stalk off righteously.

Hmm. Life. I love how it prevents us from clutching any belief for too long, before mashing it into porridge and force-feeding it back to us piecemeal.

People care more about their dogs than they do their fellow humans! The implication in this outburst is that we should save all humans first, and then move onto the animals, and then the trees, in that order. The statement is founded on extremely dubious logic, namely that there is a hierarchy of importance in which humans reign at the top. The thing is, the entire premise of hierarchy is a man-made fantasy, not a truth. And it's the reason we're in the environmental and social mess that we are. Because it's nonsense. From a universal perspective, a human is no more or less valuable or worthy of existence than an ant or a tree. When we've killed every ant and tree, we will understand this truth wholly and profoundly.

Still, whatever our philosophical and moral standpoints, in reality the personal always trumps the ideological. When we interact with something, *anything*, a physical, energetic and emotional connection is formed. If personal connection is experienced on a daily basis, the connection becomes a bond which is painful to sever. And once that happens ideologies and logic fly out of the window faster than British politicians are currently vacating leadership posts. This is where dogs are rather more switched on than humans, because as a species they've worked that out.

Truly I have no idea how it happened, but by some devilish crook of evolutionary genius my dog managed to sneak her way so deep into my heart. I am as attached to her as most people are to their children. Certainly, I've spent many a star-studded night pondering why. The truth is, despite all the fear-mongering, terrorising, morale-wrecking and cynicism-spawning agents about us, we humans just love to love. Even when we shut out the world and run up a hill, we are craving it. Searching it out. Like a mirage in a desert, we see it here, there and everywhere. Because we know it's within us, we can't help but project it. Anything can be the mirror, or engage in that feedback loop.

First I found love in the dirt of this land. Then I inhaled it from the trees and the bugs. Later I felt it towards my neighbours Celal and Dudu. Finally three years ago, Rotty the dog appeared. With a grin and a tail wag, she scooped out a cubbyhole in my heart, and curled happily up within it. Yes it felt good. So good.

And then she fell sick...

Three weeks ago, a parasite took over my little Rotty and attacked her internal organs. She grew thinner and thinner. Blood and puss poured out of her nose. Her rib cage swelled. She gave up walking.

"Have you had a dog before?" the vet said with measured deliberation, as I stood stroking her paw in the clinic.

"No," I said. "She's my one and only." It didn't escape me that the vet looked away.

I left the clinic in tears and with a prognosis of fifty-fifty. Suddenly from one day to the next the *Nowhere* was yawning before me again. It was a well of nothing. A vast all-obliterating lightlessness. Slowly I began swimming through it, stroke by heavy stroke. The days passed. Rotty deteriorated. And the next thing I knew it was Sunday the 26th June. Smoke was bubbling over the pine ridge beyond my land. The valley was on fire.

"Hello, Kerry! I'm here." I snapped my head back to see my saviour-friend peering in my window. I waved before spinning round and gaping yet again at the smoke. It was no longer dark grey but an awful moiling brown. I took a deep breath. Then the two of us quickly and furiously shipped my life out of The Mud and into her Toyota Corolla.

Soon enough we were driving out of The Mud. The Toyota chomped at the dusty incline of my track, struggling to digest the slope. With Rotty curled on the back seat and two rucksacks in the boot, I watched the roof of my home disappear from view. Beyond it flames appeared on the horizon.

I gritted my teeth and prepared to lose it all. Because let's face it, it wouldn't be the first time.

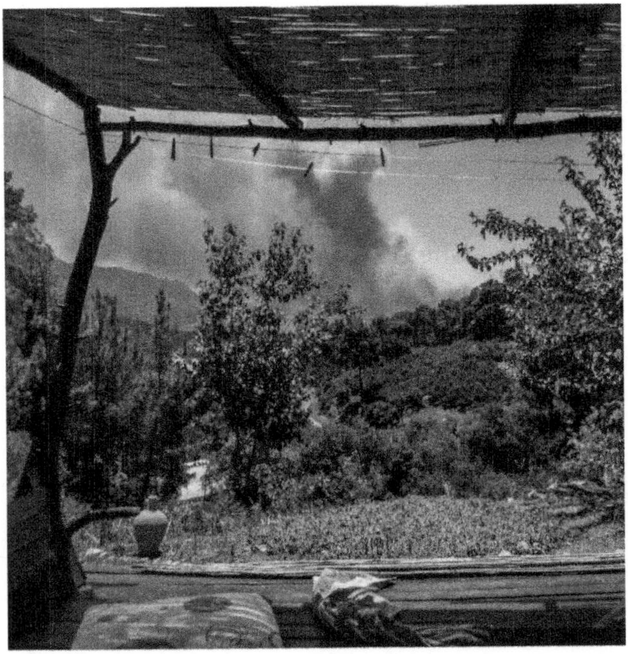

Mud Miracles

July 2016

"If the house has burned down, I'll go to India." Zeynep, was curled next to me on a floating wooden platform. She lives in a wooden cabin at the lower side of the forest bordering my house. Mountain spring water gushed below us, a cool, splashing solace. "Oh no! I left my passport in the house!" she said, slapping a delicate hand to her forehead.

It was the Sunday of the fire, and along with a good few in the valley, we had fled to a series of trout restaurants on water. Frankly, in the panic it seemed the safest place to wait. Zeynep's cat was scrunched in a plastic crate in front of us. Rotty the sick dog was lolling unhappily by the river, nose oozing. The platform was a raft, an open-air Noah's Ark.

"Ah, you can get a new passport. It's not hard," I said, and wondered what *I* would do if my house was now a charred heap of clay. Go to England? Find a van and drive? But what about Rotty? She really was too sick to move.

A waiter arrived and shunted plates around. We stared aghast at the heaving table of food in front of us. No one was in the mood to eat.

The trill of a phone sounded. It was incongruously cheery on this most heavy of days. Zeynep fumbled in her bag and picked out her mobile.

There was a silence. Then a nod. "Really? Are you sure?" She spoke slowly, curls bobbing.

Once the call was over, she pulled her sunglasses from her face, and looked at me. "The wind changed at the last minute apparently, and the fire jumped the road and over to Musa mountain."

"You're kidding?"

"Nope. We've been saved. For now. We'll give it an hour and then we'll go home.

And just as quickly as my home was snatched away, it was handed straight back to me. But I had already let it go. Perhaps that was the design.

That night, I returned to my mud home and slept, albeit it fitfully beneath the stars. The smell of smoke scratched at the inside of my nose. Musa mountain burned on, the fires gouging orange holes out of the darkness like satanic torches. Rotty the dog wheezed and puked beside me, the parasite inside her wreaking some invisible havoc. She was no more than a basket of fur-covered bones. And I felt oddly bitter. Because if there had been a choice between my dog and the house, I'd have burned that house myself.

The next morning the temperature dropped. But the humidity was a clammy veil that clung to everything. I stepped into my kitchen dragging Rotty behind me. For the second week running I cracked an egg in a glass. Stooping, I pried apart her canine mouth and poured the egg in. I wondered if Rotty could talk, whether she would tell me to back off, to let her die. She swallowed the egg with a blink and a gurgle.

Rotty's parasite required a harsh chemical treatment, one not available in Turkey and which necessitated an extensive amount of wheeler-dealing to obtain. A week earlier, thanks to connections in the animal protection world, my local animal welfare group located a bottle, and worked round the clock to get it to me. It had arrived in a mysterious package at my vet a few days prior. I had driven to collect it on my motorbike feeling I was in possession of some secret cure for cancer.

I hated administering that poison. Rotty hated taking it. But after a week of being deep fried in a 40-degrees-in-the-shade heat wave, the upheaval of the forest fire, plus the unexpected sorrow I experienced for my dog, I was incapable of any reasonable decision. Thus, I followed the mainstream advice. Rotty was to drink this poisonous elixir for 28 days non-stop. Any failure to complete the cycle would mean the parasite would gain resistance, and she would probably die.

Around midnight the next night, Rotty and I climbed under the mosquito net and onto my gazebo. I had just administered the poison. My little dog slumped onto the carpet and promptly vomited all over it. I was so tired, so in dire need of sleep, I turfed her out of the net. I heard her next to the platform, coughing and spluttering.

A few hours later, at the crack of dawn I awoke. Sitting bolt upright, I peered through the mesh hunting the shape of my dog. But I couldn't see her. Scrambling out of my duvet, I clawed at the netting, throwing it over my head. I scanned the land. No sign of my dog. A well of panic opened inside me, fathomless and murky with the faint but lingering whiff of death. I started to run, this way and that, hunting for a tuft of fur, the brush of her tail, an ear. There was nothing.

The sun pushed up, pouring its heat over the treetops in a burning torrent. Breathing hard, I ran to

Dudu. This was Rotty's favourite haunt, though I simply couldn't envisage how she could have made it all the way across the orchard. She could hardly walk.

"No, she hasn't been here. If she had, she'd be sitting right there in front of the gate wagging her tail." Dudu pulled a plastic stool out and poured me a glass of water. "Perhaps she wandered off and fell." She patted me on the shoulder sympathetically.

Fell. The thought took but seconds to spawn a family of terrible imaginings. I sat down and burst into tears. "If she doesn't turn up by tonight, she'll have missed her medicine. She's so sick. She'll *die*," I sobbed.

Within ten minutes I had left Dudu's. When I pulled the gate it scraped on the concrete, and I caught Dudu's expression, one of utter dismay.

As the sun thundered over the eastern half of the sky, I began the greatest dog hunt my valley has seen. I have no idea how many kilometres I walked that day, but it must have been a good ten at least. Charging over the rocky landscape, I crawled through brambles, stumbled into ditches, and shinned down every water gulch I could find. No Rotty. My smock stuck to me. My trousers turned from purple to dark brown.

The sun burned westward and the shadows stretched ominously. I carried on searching. As evening spread its gloom over the vale, my heart began to crack. I phoned my local healer friend. "She's gone. She's gone!" I spluttered into the mobile. My friend agreed to treat her from afar.

Finally at 9 pm on Wednesday night, I fell under the mosquito net and onto my bed. The exhaustion pulled at every muscle. But I slept little. As the sky turned from black to grey, dread plumbed my guts. Rotty had missed her medicine. The parasite now possessed an advantage. But perhaps that was no longer the urgency. Perhaps she had broken a limb somewhere and was slowly dehydrating.

Three days passed and they opened and closed like heavy, rusty gates. I spent most of them, machete in hand, going not-so-quietly barmy. Sometimes I enlisted friends to the cause and we hacked through the area searching each tiny goat trail. But each day ended exactly like the first. Once night had strangled the last drop of light out of the sky, I would collapse under my mosquito net, whimpering on and off.

At last I gave up. Three full days without food or medicine in temperatures over 40 degrees was hopeless. I made a little funeral for Rotty and said my goodbyes. I honestly didn't know anyone could feel so much grief for a dog. It stretched on and on as far as I could see, a bleak and colourless moor without so much as a rock of meaning or a peak of hope. I no longer wanted to travel Europe in a van without my furry companion. I no longer wanted to make mud homes. All had been subsumed into the Nowhere again.

Yet even there, I could sense something else. It was far, far away. Like the faintest glimmer of dawn at the farthest most point on the horizon. A strange sort of liberation. Because when it's all gone, you are free. Free to be anything or anyone you please.

Four days and nights after Rotty had left, I cleared out her things; pillows, leashes, bones, and stuffed them all in a bag ready for the dustbin. Her kennel squatted there mocking me. I placed some flowers in a bowl of water, and laid them inside, so at least I had something new to look at instead of thinking about her face poking out.

It was one in the afternoon. Scorching. I walked into my house and turned my computer on ready to broadcast this miserable news on Facebook. The computer whirred and flicked to life. Then my phone began ringing. I almost ignored it. Absently, I pulled it toward me and spied Zeynep's name.

"Hello?" I spoke tentatively into the speaker.

A heightened voice poured into my ear. Zeynep was nearly screeching with excitement. "Kerry, Rotty's *here*! I've looked three times because I couldn't believe my eyes. But she's here. Sitting under one of my bushes!"

It took a moment for me to find words. When I did I hurled them into the phone in random clumps. "You're kidding! Oh God...! I'm coming...*Now*!"

Five minutes later I was staring at my pup in utter disbelief. She was flaked out in the shade wagging her tail. On inspection I saw she was skinny and had scraped her leg somewhere. But apart from that? I had to say she looked healthier than when she left. Her nose was completely clean. No puss or blood. And it was gleaming wet.

Once again, within a week, life gave back what it seemed to snatch away. As if to remind me how tenuous it all is. And that within this all-obliterating chaos, miracles continue to swirl.

My vet was so happy to hear of Rotty's return, he drove up to the mud home to give her some intravenous assistance.

"She hasn't eaten a thing, but she must have found water somewhere," he said feeling each inch of her abdomen and squeezing her flesh between his fingers. And I smiled at the serum bag hanging from one of the wooden limbs of my gazebo.

"What's her chance of survival?" I asked. But I was calm now. Because she was home. And I'd already given her a funeral, so everything from here on out a gift.

The vet inhaled and exhaled. "Honestly, I don't know. It's all about her liver. If that recovers, she'll be OK. And you'll know if the liver is healing, because she'll start eating. She's fighting. You're fighting. But it's anyone's guess."

Four more days passed. I should have ordered another bottle of the poison. But my heart wasn't in it. If she was going to die, let her die in peace, I said to myself. And I swear she winked at me when I uttered those words. But she refused to eat. I tried everything; fresh meat, eggs, fish, milk. She was beyond disinterested.

Then suddenly, she deteriorated. She was listless. Her eyes distant. This time, however, I had reached a smoother plateau of acceptance. No more chemicals. No more forcing. Perhaps she'd just come back to say goodbye. Besides, now I believed in miracles again, so I decided to call on the Great Unknown, the mysterious and unprovable.

"Can you give her one final healing?" I asked my healer friend over the phone, as the sun slipped behind Grandmother Olive.

"Sure, I'll let you know as soon as I'm done," she said.

At 7 pm a message pinged into my phone to say the session was over. At 8 pm I placed a small bowl of liver in front of Rotty. And to my complete amazement she stood up, albeit shakily, and chomped down the lot.

She has eaten every day since.

What a garden of surprises our muddy planet is. Things live and die, and rise from the ashes. Fires can randomly change their course. A dog returns from the dead. A teacher might lose her way and camp on a hill, only to wind up building herself a mud home. Five years later she hears the Wisdom Carob whisper. "Let go of everything," it says. She doesn't want to. Because her space is intoxicating. Precious. Then the bulldozers come. She wavers. The fire comes. Her dog nearly dies. She acts. The morning she goes online to put her house up for sale, she learns there has been an attempted coup. So she waits two days. Posts the ad. 45,000 people visit the page in three days...

And as darkness rolls through this beautiful land, it's not hard to see why The Mud Home attracted so many. The diamonds of this country are right. It's time to run to the hills.

Life on planet Earth is a wilderness unto itself. A Great, sometimes terrifying, Unknown. Yet within that chaos there is a road. It winds this way and that, through forests and vales, leading us to safety. But that road isn't tarmac. It's made of dirt. Or earth. Sometimes even mud.

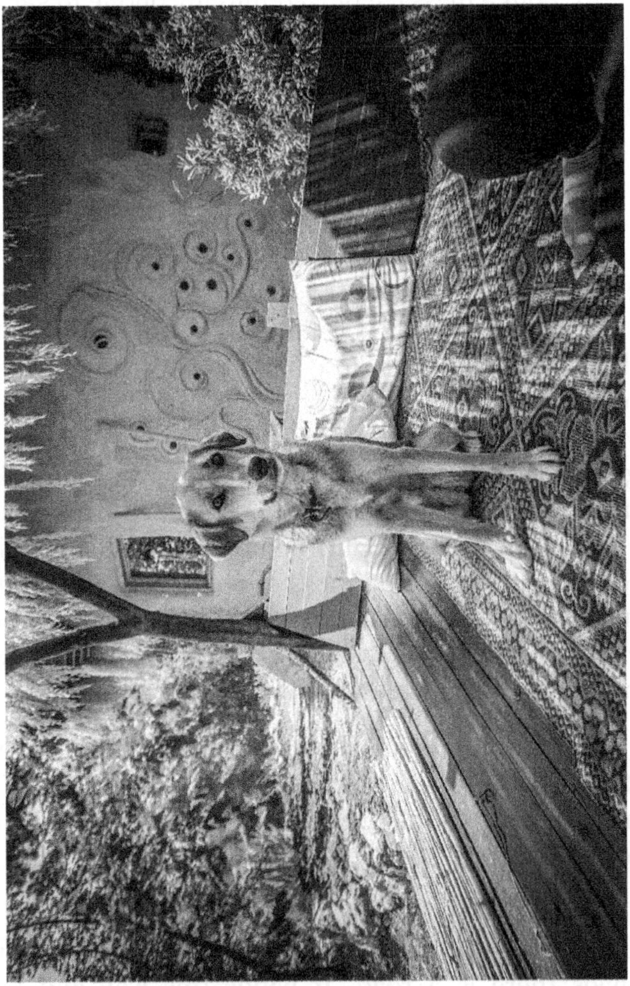

A New Witch

August 2016

The last six weeks have been merciless. The dragon of summer has awoken. And it's on the rampage, hurling its fiery breath down the valley, stamping its hot, horned feet on our earth, flattening us all.

Yes it has been one long bombardment; I have run from a forest fire, my dog died only to rise again like Lazarus, Istanbul airport was bombed, Britain voted to leave the EU, and we here in Turkey suffered an attempted coup. All this in temperatures that broil and bake and scorch us into twitching scraps of desiccated flesh.

If I am navigating the path through the flames with any ease at all, it's because of one thing. My land. My marvel-packed patch of Gaia. I am in awe. Brimming with gratitude. Because the miracles and angels just keep on raining down, extinguishing the flames and soothing the burns.

But dear land. You have changed hands. There's a new mud witch now.

It all began on Friday 14th July, the night I finally completed the advert for my house. I breathed deeply under a swelling moon when I hit the publish button, for the ad was equivalent to saying goodbye. To leaving. The heat pulsed tenaciously through the darkness. The air weighed me down. I hesitated, not quite daring yet to share the advert on social media.

The next morning I awoke early to post my announcement. But I failed again. Because there had been an attempted coup.

Here on Mud Mountain that bloody upheaval was invisible. There were no tanks or helicopters or lynch mobs nestled within the folds of the Lycian mountains. Yet even I sensed the tension. It was pulled taut over the fabric of the land like some sort of insidious shrink wrap. I've lived in this country for almost twenty years. I speak the language fluently. It is the place I have for two decades called home. We've had our excitements before, our peculiarly Turkish bloodless 'coups' where the army has arrested an ultra-conservative, called an election, and business resumes as usual. But this was far more sinister. For the first time a chill stole through me. Chaos felt close. Too close.

Overnight, the beaches cleared as each of Turkey's civil servants were called back to their posts. The expressions of the locals here dropped limp in the face of disappearing incomes. An eerie silence slid along the coast. And it hung there like the dank air from a long forgotten tomb.

But I know Turkey. For better or worse, these things are soon swept under the nearest hand-woven rug. I waited two days for the dust to settle. Then I breathed again. Opening my laptop, I turned it on and posted my ad.

It was a bleak type of perfect timing. Within days I had so many enquiries I couldn't keep track of them. Because the open-eyed have begun exiting the city, and even the country itself. I can't say I blame them.

Within days, the first viewers of my mud home appeared at the base of my track: A couple from Istanbul stepped out of a car and into the mud. Yes mud. Because very peculiarly it had poured with rain the entire morning, and the steam now rose from the hill creases to swallow the view.

The woman was young. Raven haired. Pretty. And her partner was a small, friendly looking fellow with erratic hair. Slowly we wandered around the plot, into the forest, down to the olive trees. The couple peered at the solar system. They didn't flinch at the composting toilet. Nor the outside kitchen. I made tea. And we chatted. Easily. Because we had much in common. Deniz concocted herbal remedies and natural beauty products. Alp worked in the music industry. And Deniz's dad was an architect fascinated by off-grid living and earthships. Soon, I was surprised to find myself having a good time.

At least two hours later the pair rose to leave. How slowly they edged towards the gate. Deniz in particular seemed stuck at the neck of the land, her dark hair dampened by the misty air. And I chuckled. Because my land is such a beguiler.

The next day Deniz phoned. "I guess I've warmed to the place. I'm interested in buying," she said. And my heart lurched.

Oh how I sobbed that night, fretting that it was all too hasty. I wondered how I should know if these were the right people. Squatting on my gazebo with the light fading, I switched on my laptop. Then I opened Facebook to snoop. But when I clicked on Deniz's profile, I blinked hard. For what should I see, but a "witch workshop" she was organising. Witch. She was a witch? Something sang inside my chest. And the pine trees rustled.

Three days later Deniz placed a deposit on the land. I was calm by then. I knew they were the right people. Incredible as it might be, I had sold my land in less than a week.

This Sunday, a roaster of a day if ever there was one, Deniz and Alp drove back to my mud home. They had come to learn the art of earth plastering. It was late afternoon. The sun dove behind the trees, but it made no difference. The wind was a type of fire that all but charred our skin. The air itself was aflame.

Quickly, I wheeled the barrow and the sieve into place. Alp ferried the earth and water over. Deniz softened the clay and mixed the plaster. And as I watched her hands stirring the mud, the feeling that bloomed within me was one of gratitude and wonder. Taking a step back, I stared over at Grandmother Olive and heard her whisper.

"You see?"

As Deniz lobbed the plaster gently at the house, and rubbed it in over one or two cracks, she smiled. Then looked up at me. "Oh," she said. "I see completely why you want to build another one."

Later, as evening wove through the trees and settled onto the slope, we hunkered down in the gazebo. The teapot was full. The conversation flowed anew.

"Once I travelled over land to India," Deniz said sipping at her tea glass.

I turned towards her, gaping in the darkness. "You travelled through Iran and Pakistan?"

"Yes," she said. "Me and a girlfriend back in 2008."

"No one does that trip," I said shaking my head a little. "No one. I did it back in 2009 the other way round. It was the hairiest and simultaneously most incredible journey of my life."

"Same here," Deniz laughed. She was a strong young woman, healthy and able. I punched her lightly on the arm and raised my tea glass to her. "Respect," I said. She fell back and grinned.

That night, Deniz and Alp slept on the gazebo with a happy Rotty the dog flaked out beside them. The stars shone their magic onto them, shifting into new patterns and collaborative shapes. And I sensed it. The slight movement of the trees. The reaching toward.

As the sun peeped over the forest the next morning, the first bars of gold light struck the earth. I spied a figure; Deniz treading slowly over the land, dark hair now plaited into a single braid. She was dressed in patterned salwars and a vest top with sunglasses perched on her head. Suddenly I was watching a younger version of myself. A new mud witch. And I just knew. She was hearing it. Feeling it.

It was 4 pm on the 8th of August that Deniz and I signed the deeds. As we sat together in the deeds office waiting for the haphazard cog of Turkish bureaucracy to grind to a conclusion, such a wave of happiness crashed over me. I felt blessed. This was all perfect. For the land. For them and for me.

"I was a bit worried in the night. I wasn't sure I could manage all the trees. And the digging. I suddenly wondered whether I could do it," Deniz said as we huddled on the uncomfortable plastic chairs. We watched the human movement behind the glass of the deeds office carefully, willing them to action.

"Don't worry, the land will help you," I confided. "If you ever feel doubt, just remember. I couldn't even bang a nail in when I moved there. I didn't know a thing."

An official barked at us from behind the glass. I met Deniz's brown eyes with my green ones. It was a good moment. Auspicious. Right.

That evening, as I lay on my gazebo with Rotty the dog panting beside me, I felt the power of this planet. The prodigiousness of it all. The unbridled love. The extraordinary. I arrived here five years ago with no money and no clue. Since then I've been inspired and supported to build a home, a thriving website, and a writing career. Suddenly I am in abundance, possessing a brand new skill set, energetically, emotionally and financially equipped for a new adventure.

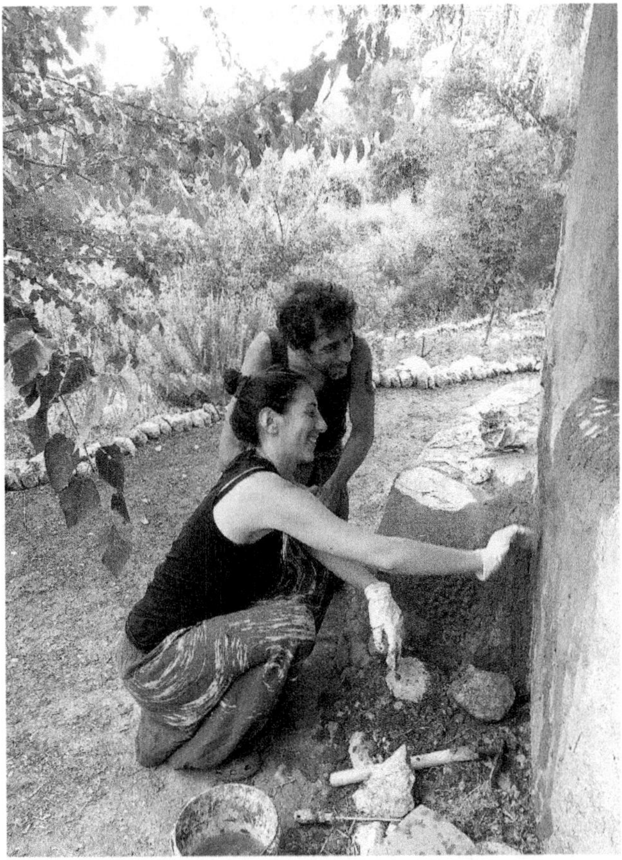

Moving Out

On the 16th September 2016 I left Mud Mountain. The sky gave no intimation of autumn. The land was sun-ravaged, the forests thirsty. Without Esra, I would never have managed.

Esra was Celal's daughter-in-law and one of the leading characters in *Mud Ball*, helping me to build my house back in 2011. Since then she had become my right hand woman. We built the shade over my platform together, the bathroom door, and half the kitchen roof, to name but a few of our creations.

Opening my door, I heard her motorbike chugging down my track. That dirt road had never improved in quality in all the five and a half years I was there. I liked its axle-pummelling potholes, and its propensity to dissolve in winter. It kept the nosey at bay.

"Helloooo!" Esra called as she pushed through the rickety gate. Rotty the dog bounded towards her.

"Oh she looks so much better!" The young woman bent to both stroke and fend off Rotty, who was bouncing and licking and squealing. She was dressed in a pair of shorts, and it was the first time I'd ever seen a village woman bare her legs. This was typical of Esra, ground-breaking as always.

I had often wondered what Esra would have become, had she chanced to be born in a middle income European family, rather than Yapraklı village in Turkey. A fast track professional? Conference organiser? PA? She could easily have run a successful business, perhaps been a corporate high flyer. Though whether she'd have been more or less fulfilled in such a life, is hard for me to say.

Indeed, it was due to Esra's advanced managerial skills, I had called upon her that penultimate day. When I procrastinate, she pushes me into action. And I *was* procrastinating. As I cleared my home, each item I packed sucked at my attention. I found myself sinking into a quicksand of stodgy memories, where I could wade on the spot for hours. The past loves to cling to our coattails. It's a heavy passenger, however. I knew I was done on Mud Mountain. I knew beyond all doubt now, I had to leave.

Free from sentimentality, Esra moved swiftly. And the cool womb of my mud home released me. I closed my eyes as she gathered my books into boxes. My clothes. My hand tools. Within two hours she had emptied my shelves.

We squinted as we stepped out of the house, the sky now a fulgent white egg we were trying to crack our way out of. Walking through the gate, the pair of us reached the dirt road. Here we spread a tarp on the dust. Then one by one, we hauled each box out of my mud home and into the sun.

As I stared at the heap of belongings, I was reminded of the day I had arrived here with a similar hillock of stuff. It's odd to see the extent of your ownership reduced to a small cluster of bags and boxes.

Soon we heard the taxi. It jolted and lurched as it eased its way down to my land. The driver braked. Opened the doors. And we began to load the vehicle. He would take it to a friend's house where it would be stored until I left Turkey.

That evening I returned to my Mud Home. This was the moment I had been dreading. There's little solace to be found in an empty house. Yet, as I stepped through the doorway and onto the juniper floor, the smell drove into me as it always does. The sweet aroma of mud and wood. The warmth and the freshness. The beauty.

Generally speaking, the houses of the modern world are soulless. They are neither constructed with love, nor care. So it is down to the owner to breathe life into these sterile carcasses, with furnishings, ornaments, paintings, décor. When these are removed, the barren soulscape of the building becomes once more apparent.

But when you build your *own* home, when you mould it with your own hands, the house itself has a soul. This was evident now, as I stood within it. Because it was just as lovely without my belongings, as it had been with them.

As I stood in front of those glass doors, the last of the light catching the mud ridges of my tree sculpture, I smiled. The thick foliage of the garden fruit trees: apricots, lemons, oranges and mulberries that I'd planted years ago, filled my windows with green life. The slope was barely visible now through the leaves. Yet the road below was clear. It swirled left and right, its meandering aesthetic carving through the heart of the pine forest, round the bend, and out of sight.

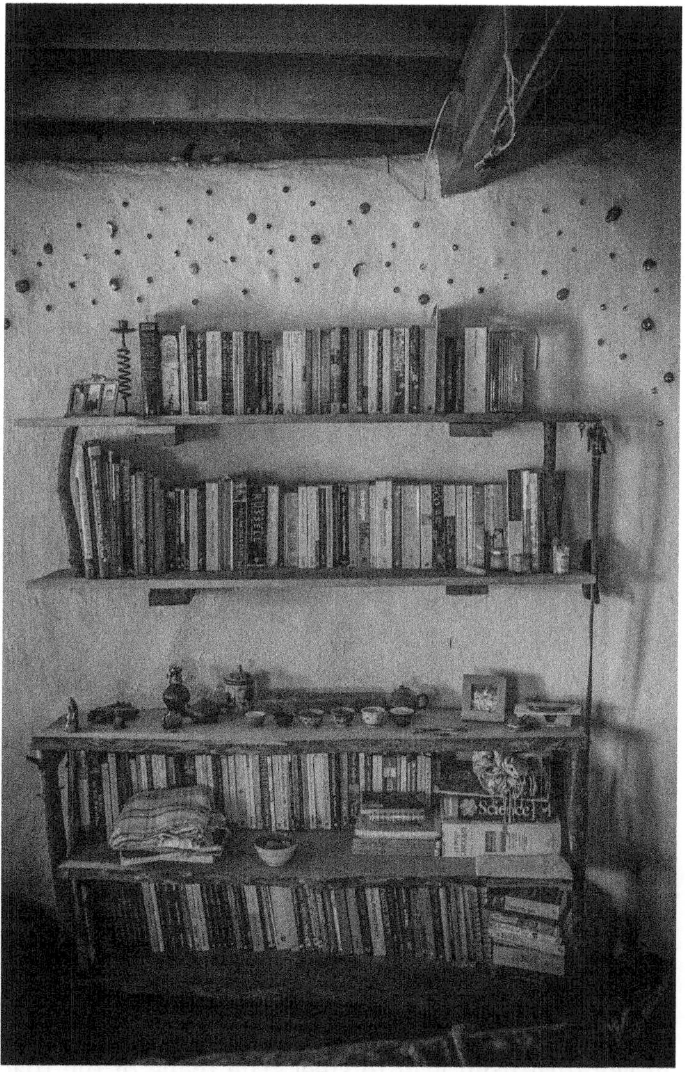
Science

The Road Ahead

November 2017

"It's a dangerous business, Frodo, going out your door. You step onto the road, and if you don't keep your feet, there's no knowing where you might be swept off to."
— **J.R.R. Tolkien, The Lord of the Rings**

Dawn can be much like dusk. Only colder. The darkness capitulates. A ridge of mountains pulls itself out of the night. Clouds distinguish themselves from the sky. And the world exists once more. It's never the same world as yesterday. The night changes everything.

The ridges I spotted as day broke on the 7th of November, were the mighty caps of the Bey Mountains. Snow hadn't reached them yet, their treeless heads were still brown. A road threaded through them. The road I was on. It plunged north-westwards to the city of Izmir, slicing through bygone cities and ancient burial mounds.

Rotty's furry head poked over the armrest. I stroked between her ears. Panting a little, she nuzzled the arm of our driver. Through the windscreen I watched bands of sky turn from lead to steel. The twine of the road grew clearer. This was my last dawn in Turkey. For a while at least. After almost twenty years, I was leaving the land of my heart. Because my heart had moved. Though where?

Twenty years is a long time. I was 26 when I moved to Turkey, a young woman very different from the mud-home building, wilderness-loving witch I am now. I married here, divorced here, moved homes, built and lost businesses. I had woven friendships, networks and communities over the years. I knew the ropes. Understood the rigging. Could make my way through the coded warrens of Turkey's various systems.

It's a lot to leave behind. More than just a mud home on a beautiful hill.

Yes. More than that.

It began with a carob tree whispering across the ravines of time, and a bulldozer growling at my fence. It began when I imagined building another home and felt a flurry inside my heart. It began when a friend of mine sent me photos of land the other side of Europe, when I cast my eye upon the Atlantic coast and sensed something inside me hungering. Yes, that's where it began.

But it has been transmuted into something else. For the world has shifted into another shape. I'm not the only one moving. Turkey is on a road too, and like me it's changed direction. One midsummer night there was this mysterious coup, and since then a good 70,000 people (at least) have been arrested. Opposition newspapers have been closed, opposition politicians arrested. It's pretty much a fait accompli. They are discussing the reintroduction of the death penalty as I write.

I no longer enter much political debate. It's too uninspiring. (And depending on where you live, too incriminating.) The serious study of a tree or a bird offers far more light than the intellectualised bickering or emotional ranting of the political domain. Besides, it's not the focus of this blog, nor my area of expertise. But for what it's worth (and it might not be worth much – though let's face it, few of the official pundits seem any more capable of prophecy) this is a snippet of my perspective from the inside.

Some say Turkey will become Iran. Others say Afghanistan. One or two are in complete denial and pretend nothing at all is happening. I seriously doubt Turkey will become Afghanistan or Iran. The leadership is far more ambitious (in case you hadn't noticed). This isn't the 1990s, either. In the new world, Turkey is financially sturdy (currently 18th largest economy in the world, with a higher GDP than Saudi Arabia and Switzerland) and in possession of some business savvy. Lest we forget, it also holds the 10th most powerful military in the world, fourth largest in NATO. Socio-economically speaking, I'd start looking vaguely in the direction of the UAE, if you want to see where Turkey's trajectory is headed. The UAE with a hefty army, a lust for importance, and a toe inside Europe.

Oh well (sigh). I expect international business will carry on as usual, regardless of human rights (Britain is already talking about trade deals with Turkey). And if you keep your head down and your mouth shut, you might just be able to pretend all is sort of alright, until they drag off your neighbour for questioning that is, or build a shopping mall in your back garden.

But for many citizens of the country, for those who can't shoehorn themselves into the narrow social constraints of what is deemed acceptable by those in power; for women, for the ethnic minorities, for the secularists, for those who adore Turkey's incredible nature, the artists, the LGBT community, child brides, anyone who wants to think outside the box and speak their mind, and for whom Tommy Hilfiger and a macchiatto simply aren't enough compensation...for them? Right now, the new Turkish dawn isn't too rosy.

This has all been brewing for years of course. But like a slow-swelling boil that finally bursts, the explosion of pus is startling. I sense something I haven't felt in Turkey since my very first visits back in the late eighties. An undercurrent of unease. And the hurried closing of mouths.

Staring through the windscreen on that early November morning, I imbibed Turkey's natural beauty one last time. The jagged upsurges of mountain rock were petering out, leaving the hills to deflate on the plains. Our jeep hummed up a gear. The sun peered over a summit, and in an instant the waves of the valley were gold-plated. The road spawned factories and conurbations. The temperature rose. Pulling off my jacket, I stretched, then reached for my bottle of water. I noted, despite this parting of ways, how inspirited I felt.

There is something inordinately therapeutic about the road. It is a continuum of reason in a mad world. A rolling sequence of reassurance. The landscape changes. Mountains disappear. Orchards flick in and out of view. Cities sprout. Flocks of birds fly overhead one minute. Fighter jets roar over the next. But the road is still there. Moving. From one place to the next. Holding your feet and guiding your soul.

The steel tube of Izmir airport pulled into view. I turned to stroke my dog still grinning on the back seat, wonderfully oblivious that she was about to fly across Europe. As we pulled up to the shiny rectangles of the departure doors, I realised something. The only other time I had set foot in Izmir airport was the first time I visited the country way back in 1988.

Smiling, I opened my passenger door. I was leaving Turkey by the same gateway I had entered almost three decades apart. Once again the lightning of coincidence was striking my path, and the scene was set for kismet. For a journey from East back to West. To new lands that whisper. New rocks with old memories. And a new Eden.

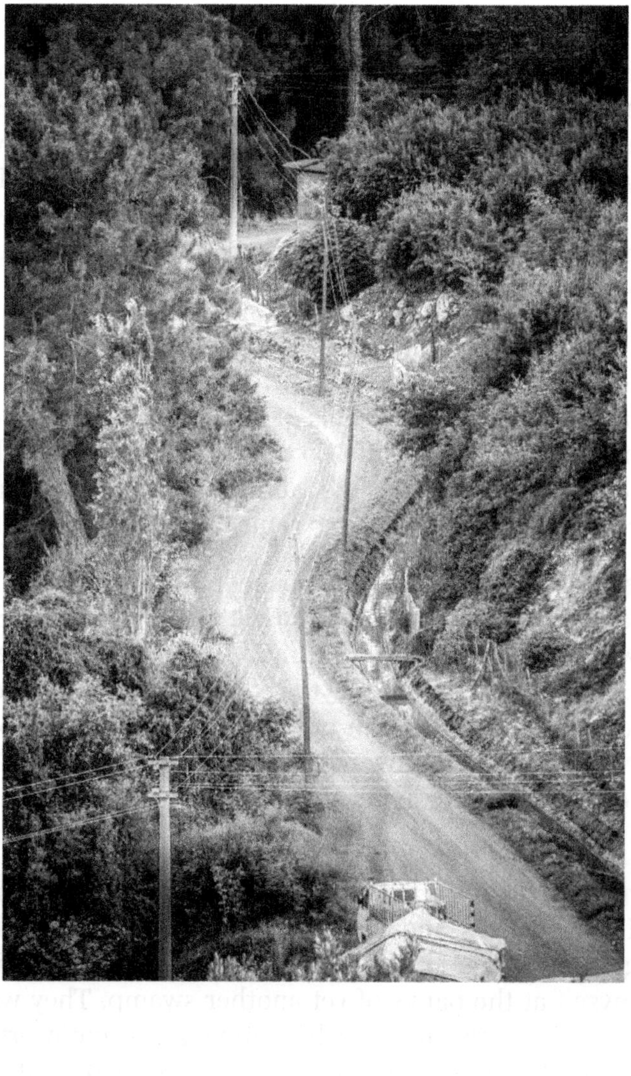

Epilogue

Things looked very different back in 2011, when I found myself, pick in hand, on my land that first day. Hacking at the ground, sweat beading on my inexpert brow, I *did* manage to clear a space for my tent before dark. But I was lost. That's why I was there. All my grand projects had gone up in smoke. I was economically challenged and burned out.

Initially, my plan (if you could call it that) was only to camp through the summer. I had no rent to pay up on Mud Mountain. No bills. It was a way of pressing the pause button on my life, so that I could work out what to do next. By the onset of autumn I assumed I'd have regained enough energy to return to my teaching job.

But strange things happened. Earthy things. My land began to whisper to me. Cast dirt spells on me. She wrapped herself around me. Dug under my 21st century skin. Without the distraction of modern 'conveniences', I began tapping into new dimensions. New powers. I discovered skills and strengths I had no idea I possessed, nor even that I desired.

The Mud transformed my entire view of life and its meaning. For the first time, I fell in love with existence. Its challenges and disputes were no longer a thick, gloomy sludge I was wading through, only to find myself at the banks of yet another swamp. They were rock faces to climb; exhilarating and empowering. Soon, I'd wake up each day in a bizarre state of excitement, not able to wait for the hours to unfold.

There's a magic to the natural world, you see. It has its own rules and its own path. When you follow it, the days become vast canvases to paint your soul upon, while the nights are starlit muses murmuring ideas from afar.

Thus a summer turned into a winter, and that turned into five more. At one point, I *did* have to return to teaching for six months to earn the money to finish my earthbag house. But the last time I worked (in the ordinary sense of the word) was 2012. I have evaded the daily grind for over four years.

Yes. It is possible to live like this. To feel like this. And no you don't need much money to do it. What you need is the courage to leave the old behind, an openness to hear the Earth speak, and to take the first step, however small. The rest will find its way to you.

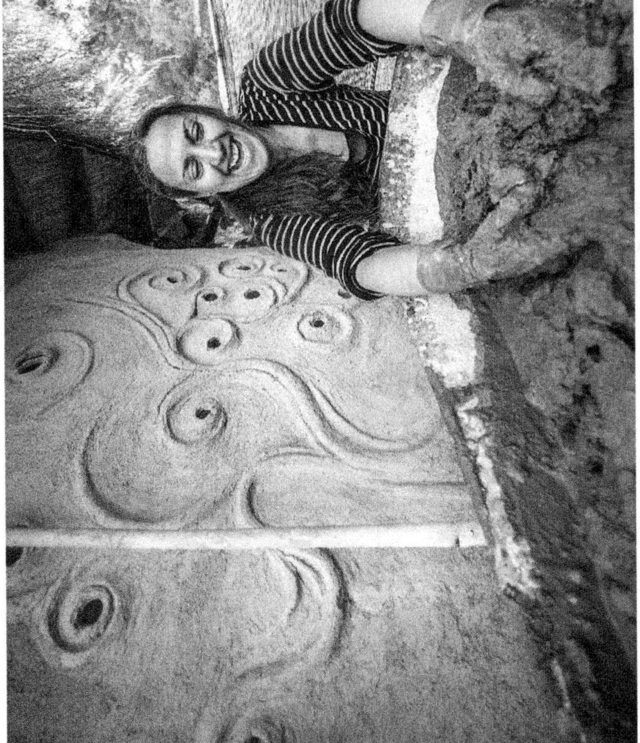

If you enjoyed this book, please leave a review at the online distributor of your choice. It will be greatly appreciated.

***

Atulya K Bingham is a natural builder and author. Her other books include: **Ayse's Trail (OBBL winner 2014)**, and **Mud Ball**, the popular true story of how she built her earthbag home.

For more information about earthbag building, living sustainably off-grid or Atulya's other way of life, go to www.themudhome.com.

You can download her Earthbag Building PDF, a step by step explanation of how she built her earthbag house from:

http://www.themudhome.com/earthbag-building.html

mud BALL

6 weeks, $6000, and plenty of dirt

How I dug myself out of the daily grind

Atulya K Bingham

"Beautifully written," **The Owner Builder Magazine**

"If you've ever fantasized about going off-grid, this book is a must read," **The Fethiye Times**

Excerpt from Mud Ball

Adnan's fastidious gaze fixed on the front wall. He stood up silently. I turned away and stared at the view. The sun was hitting the needles of the thousands and thousands of pine trees, and they fluttered in the breeze like tall, green peacocks.

'Kerry, we have a problem.'

I groaned. I was starting to feel like the ground control supervisor of Apollo 13. Where did all these damn problems keep sprouting from? They were like wayward eyebrow hairs. Was there no end to them? I turned to Adnan. 'What now?' I snapped.

'I have no idea how we missed this. You guys were measuring with a plumb line when I was gone, right?'

'Of course!' I stood up indignantly. After the ubiquitous translation, Esra's eyes drew together outraged. '*Tabi ki!*' she said in Turkish, repeating exactly what I'd said.

'Well, I guess you weren't doing it, like top to bottom. Because if I let the plumb line drop from the top of *this* part of the wall...' And here Adnan climbed up on to our plank scaffold, then dropped the stone on the string that was our plumb line. 'You can see it's like...hell, Kerry! It's a good ten centimetres out! The front wall is *leaning*. Holy shit...this *can't* be good!'

I managed a good two minutes of stoicism before my self-control splintered. The definitive crack of my mood was probably heard as far as Dudu's house. I was simply too tired. Resting my head in my hands I pouted, suddenly feeling an irrational urge to locate a sledgehammer and start whacking slews out of the wall. As it happened, even if I had found a sledgehammer, the wall would have stayed standing. That's the way it is with earthbag roundhouses. I stood up and kicked the bag stand. After growling at the offending bulge for a minute or two, I plucked the tape measure from its nail in the shed. 'Alright, let's measure it!' I barked.

As humans are always more eager to learn of disaster than triumph, the team crowded round eagerly for a closer look. Esra was chewing her thumb while Adnan held the plumb line. I measured the distance from the base of the wall. It was near on 15 centimetres out. Sitting back on my heels I started to feel marginally persecuted. Obviously this was terrible. Walls are not made to lean. We needed a solution.

The Mud Home